Multithreading in C# 5.0 Cookbook

Over 70 recipes to help you learn asynchronous and
parallel programming with C# 5.0 quickly and efficiently

Eugene Agafonov

PUBLISHING

BIRMINGHAM - MUMBAI

Multithreading in C# 5.0 Cookbook

First published: November 2013

Production Reference: 1191113

Published by Packt Publishing Ltd.
Livery Place
35 Livery Street
Birmingham B3 2PB, UK.

ISBN 978-1-84969-764-4

www.packtpub.com

Cover Image by Aniket Sawant (aniket_sawant_photography@hotmail.com)

Credits

Author

Eugene Agafonov

Reviewers

Mickael Ferrer

Chad McCallum

Philip Pierce

Acquisition Editor

James Jones

Lead Technical Editor

Chalini Snega Victor

Technical Editors

Menza Mathew

Pooja Nair

Copy Editors

Brandt D'Mello

Mradula Hegde

Gladson Monteiro

Sayanee Mukherjee

Aditya Nair

Karuna Narayanan

Kirti Pai

Laxmi Subramanian

Project Coordinator

Apeksha Chitnis

Proofreader

Clyde Jenkins

Indexer

Marriammal Chettiyar

Production Coordinator

Pooja Chiplunkar

Cover Work

Pooja Chiplunkar

About the Author

Eugene Agafonov leads a web development department at ABBYY, and lives and works in Moscow. He has over 15 years of professional experience in software development and started to work with C# from the time it was in its beta version. He is a Microsoft MVP in ASP.NET since 2006, and he often speaks at local software development conferences, such as TechEd Russia, about cutting-edge technologies in the Modern Web and server-side application development. His main professional interests are cloud-based software architecture, scalability, and reliability. Eugene is a huge fan of football and plays the guitar with a local rock band. You can reach him at his personal blog eugeneagafonov.com or with his twitter handle @eugene_agafonov.

About the Reviewers

Mickael Ferrer is a geek who has played with a lot of technologies through the years; He is the jack of all trades, but master of none.He specialized in .Net and C# development, in particular, for extending Excel.He spent much of his short professional career in the financial industry as a front-office developer.He recently started a self-employed training business for .Net developers.He randomly writes stuff on his technical blog at `pragmateek.com`

Chad McCallum is a Saskatchewan computer geek and an ASP.NET MVP with over seven years of .NET experience. After graduating from the Computer Systems Technology course at SIAST in Saskatoon, he picked up contracting until he could pester iQmetrix to give him a job, where he's been for the last seven years. He had a brief stint in Vancouver, working on interactive retail software. Since then, he's come back to Regina, SK, where he's started HackREGINA, a hackathon organization aimed at strengthening the developer community while coding and drinking beer. Somehow, between his real-life job and sleep, he managed to publish a Pluralsight course on 10 Ways to Build Web Services in .NET. His current focus is on single-page applications with JavaScript. Between random app ideas, he tries to learn a new technology every week; you can see the results on `www.rtigger.com`.

Philip Pierce is a software developer with twenty years of experience in mobile, web, desktop, and server development, database design and management, and game development. His background includes creating A.I. for games and business software, converting AAA games among various platforms, developing multithreaded applications, and creating patented client/server communication technologies.

Philip has won several hackathons, including Best Mobile App at the AT&T Developer Summit 2013, and a runner up for Best Windows 8 App at PayPal's Battlethon Miami. His most recent project was converting Rail Rush and Temple Run 2 from the Android platform to Arcade platforms.

Philip's portfolios can be found at `http://www.rocketgamesmobile.com` and `http://www.philippiercedeveloper.com`.

www.PacktPub.com

Support files, eBooks, discount offers and more

You might want to visit www.PacktPub.com for support files and downloads related to your book.

Did you know that Packt offers eBook versions of every book published, with PDF and ePub files available? You can upgrade to the eBook version at www.PacktPub.com and as a print book customer, you are entitled to a discount on the eBook copy. Get in touch with us at service@packtpub.com for more details.

At www.PacktPub.com, you can also read a collection of free technical articles, sign up for a range of free newsletters and receive exclusive discounts and offers on Packt books and eBooks.

http://PacktLib.PacktPub.com

Do you need instant solutions to your IT questions? PacktLib is Packt's online digital book library. Here, you can access, read and search across Packt's entire library of books.

Why Subscribe?

- ▸ Fully searchable across every book published by Packt
- ▸ Copy and paste, print and bookmark content
- ▸ On demand and accessible via web browser

Free Access for Packt account holders

If you have an account with Packt at www.PacktPub.com, you can use this to access PacktLib today and view nine entirely free books. Simply use your login credentials for immediate access.

To my dearly beloved wife Helen and son Nikita

Table of Contents

Preface

Not so long ago, a typical personal computer CPU had only one computing core, and the power consumption was enough to cook fried eggs on it. In 2005, Intel introduced its first multiple-core CPU, and since then computers started developing in a different direction. Low power consumption and a number of computing cores became more important than a row computing core performance. This lead to programming paradigm changes as well. Now we need to learn how to use all CPU cores effectively to achieve the best performance, and at the same time, save battery power by running only the programs we need at a particular time. Besides that, we need to program server applications in a way to use multiple CPU cores or even multiple computers as efficiently as possible to support as many users as we can.

To be able to create such applications, you have to learn to use multiple CPU cores in your programs effectively. If you use the Microsoft .NET development platform and C# programming language, this book will be a perfect starting point for programming applications that have good performance and responsiveness.

The purpose of this book is to provide you with a step-by-step guide for multithreading and parallel programming in C#. We will start with the basic concepts, going through more and more advanced topic based on the information from previous chapters, and end with real-world parallel programming patterns and Windows Store application samples.

What this book covers

Chapter 1, *Threading Basics*, introduces basic operations with threads in C#. It explains what a thread is, the pros and cons of using threads, and other important thread aspects.

Chapter 2, *Thread Synchronization*, describes thread interaction details. You will learn why we need to coordinate threads together and the different ways of organizing thread coordination.

Chapter 3, *Using a Thread Pool*, explains a thread pool concept. It shows how to use a thread pool, how to work with asynchronous operations, and good and bad practices of using a thread pool.

Chapter 4, Using Task Parallel Library, is a deep dive into a Task Parallel Library framework. This chapter outlines every important aspect of TPL, including tasks combination, exceptions management, and operations cancellation.

Chapter 5, Using C# 5.0, explains in detail the new C# 5.0 feature – asynchronous methods. You will find out what async and await keywords mean, how to use them in different scenarios, and how await works under the hood.

Chapter 6, Using Concurrent Collections, describes standard data structures for parallel algorithms included in the .NET Framework. It goes through sample programming scenarios for each data structure.

Chapter 7, Using PLINQ, is a deep dive into the Parallel LINQ infrastructure. The chapter describes task and data parallelism, parallelizing a LINQ query, tweaking parallelism options, partitioning a query, and aggregating parallel query result.

Chapter 8, Reactive Extensions, explains how and when to use the Reactive Extensions framework. You will learn how to compose events and how to perform a LINQ query against an event sequence.

Chapter 9, Using Asynchronous I/O, covers in detail the asynchronous I/O process including files, networks, and database scenarios.

Chapter 10, Parallel Programming Patterns, outlines the common parallel programming problem solutions.

Chapter 11, There's More, covers the aspects of programming asynchronous applications for Windows 8. You will learn how to work with Windows 8 asynchronous APIs, and how to perform background work in Windows Store applications.

What you need for this book

For most of the recipes, you will need Microsoft Visual Studio Express 2012 for Windows Desktop. Recipes in Chapter 11 will require Windows 8 and Microsoft Visual Studio Express 2012 for Windows 8 to compile Windows Store applications.

Who this book is for

Multithreading in C# 5.0 Cookbook is written for existing C# developers with little or no background in multithreading, and asynchronous and parallel programming. The book covers these topics from basic concepts to complicated programming patterns and algorithms using C# and .NET ecosystem.

Conventions

In this book, you will find a number of styles of text that distinguish among different kinds of information. Here are some examples of these styles, and an explanation of their meaning.

Code words in text are shown as follows: " When we construct a thread, an instance of the `ThreadStart` or `ParameterizedThreadStart` delegate is passed to the constructor."

A block of code is set as follows:

```
static void PrintNumbers()
{
  Console.WriteLine("Starting...");
  for (int i = 1; i < 10; i++)
  {
    Console.WriteLine(i);
  }
}
```

New terms and **important words** are shown in bold. Words that you see on the screen, in menus or dialog boxes for example, appear in the text like this: "Start Visual Studio 2012. Create a new C# **Console Application** project."

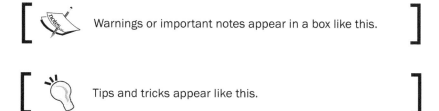

Warnings or important notes appear in a box like this.

Tips and tricks appear like this.

Reader feedback

Feedback from our readers is always welcome. Let us know what you think about this book—what you liked or may have disliked. Reader feedback is important for us to develop titles that you really get the most out of.

To send us general feedback, simply send an e-mail to `feedback@packtpub.com`, and mention the book title via the subject of your message.

If there is a topic in which you have expertise, and you are interested in either writing or contributing to a book, see our author guide on www.packtpub.com/authors.

Customer support

Now that you are the proud owner of a Packt book, we have a number of things to help you to get the most from your purchase.

Downloading the example code

You can download the example code files for all Packt books you have purchased from your account at `http://www.packtpub.com`. If you purchased this book elsewhere, you can visit `http://www.packtpub.com/support` and register to have the files e-mailed directly to you.

Errata

Although we have taken every care to ensure the accuracy of our content, mistakes do happen. If you find a mistake in one of our books—maybe a mistake in the text or the code—we would be grateful if you would report this to us. By doing so, you can save other readers from frustration and help us improve subsequent versions of this book. If you find any errata, please report them by visiting `http://www.packtpub.com/submit-errata`, selecting your book, clicking on the **errata submission form** link, and entering the details of your errata. Once your errata are verified, your submission will be accepted and the errata will be uploaded on our website, or added to any list of existing errata, under the Errata section of that title. Any existing errata can be viewed by selecting your title from `http://www.packtpub.com/support`.

Piracy

Piracy of copyright material on the Internet is an ongoing problem across all media. At Packt, we take the protection of our copyright and licenses very seriously. If you come across any illegal copies of our works, in any form, on the Internet, please provide us with the location address or website name immediately so that we can pursue a remedy.

Please contact us at `copyright@packtpub.com` with a link to the suspected pirated material.

We appreciate your help in protecting our authors, and our ability to bring you valuable content.

Questions

You can contact us at `questions@packtpub.com` if you are having a problem with any aspect of the book, and we will do our best to address it.

1
Threading Basics

In this chapter, we will cover the basic tasks for working with threads in C#.
You will learn about:

- ▸ Creating a thread in C#
- ▸ Pausing a thread
- ▸ Making a thread wait
- ▸ Aborting a thread
- ▸ Determining thread state
- ▸ Thread priority
- ▸ Foreground and background threads
- ▸ Passing parameters to a thread
- ▸ Locking with a C# lock keyword
- ▸ Locking with a Monitor construct
- ▸ Handling exceptions

Introduction

At some point of time in the past, the common computer had only one computing unit and could not execute several computing tasks simultaneously. However, operating systems could already work with multiple programs simultaneously, implementing the concept of multitasking. To prevent the possibility of one program taking control of the CPU, forever causing other applications and the operating system itself to hang, the operating systems had to split a physical computing unit across a few virtualized processors in some way and give a certain amount of computing power to each executing program. Moreover, an operating system must always have priority access to the CPU and should be able to prioritize CPU access to different programs. A thread is an implementation of this concept. It could be considered a virtual processor given to the one specific program that runs it independently.

Remember that a thread consumes a significant amount of operating system resources. Trying to share one physical processor across many threads will lead to a situation where an operating system is busy just managing threads instead of running programs.

Therefore, while it was possible to enhance computer processors, making them execute more and more commands per second, working with threads was usually an operating system task. There was no sense in trying to compute some tasks in parallel on a single-core CPU because it would take more time than running those computations sequentially. However, when processors started to have more computing cores, older programs could not take advantage of this because they just used one processor core.

To use a modern processor's computing power effectively, it is very important to be able to compose a program in a way that it can use more than one computing core, which leads to organizing it as several threads communicating and synchronizing with each other.

The recipes in this chapter will focus on performing some very basic operations with threads in the C# language. We will cover a thread's lifecycle, which includes creating, suspending, making a thread wait, and aborting a thread, and then we will go through basic synchronization techniques.

Creating a thread in C#

Throughout the following recipes, we will use Visual Studio 2012 as the main tool to write multithreaded programs in C#. This recipe will show you how to create a new C# program and use threads in it.

There are free Visual Studio 2012 Express editions, which can be downloaded from the Microsoft website. We will need Visual Studio 2012 Express for Windows Desktop for most of the examples and Visual Studio 2012 Express for Windows 8 for Windows 8-specific recipes.

Getting ready

To work through this recipe, you will need Visual Studio 2012. There are no other prerequisites. The source code for this recipe can be found at `BookSamples\Chapter1\Recipe1`.

Downloading the example code

You can download the example code files for all Packt books you have purchased through your account at `http://www.packtpub.com`. If you purchased this book elsewhere, you can visit `http://www.packtpub.com/support` and register to have the files e-mailed directly to you.

How to do it...

To understand how to create a new C# program and use threads in it, perform the following steps:

1. Start Visual Studio 2012. Create a new C# **Console Application** project.
2. Make sure that the project uses .NET Framework 4.0 or higher version.

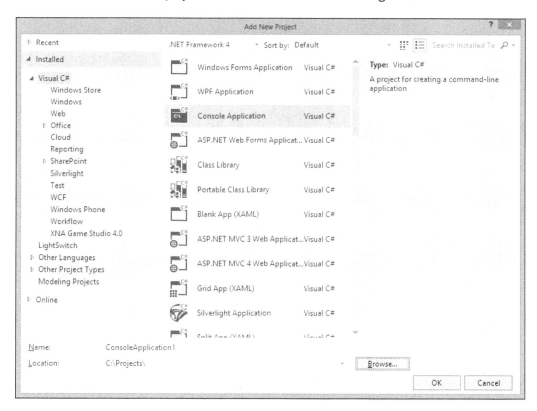

3. In the `Program.cs` file add the following `using` directives:

```
using System;
using System.Threading;
```

4. Add the following code snippet below the `Main` method:

```
static void PrintNumbers()
{
  Console.WriteLine("Starting...");
  for (int i = 1; i < 10; i++)
  {
    Console.WriteLine(i);
  }
}
```

5. Add the following code snippet inside the `Main` method:

```
Thread t = new Thread(PrintNumbers);
t.Start();
PrintNumbers();
```

6. Run the program. The output will be something like:

How it works...

In steps 1 and 2 we created a simple console application in C# using .Net Framework version 4.0. Then in step 3 we included the namespace `System.Threading`, which contains all the types needed for the program.

An instance of a program is being executed can be referred to as a process. A process consists of one or more threads. This means that when we run a program, we always have one main thread that executes the program code.

In step 4 we defined the method `PrintNumbers`, which will be used in both the main and newly created threads. Then in step 5, we created a thread that runs `PrintNumbers`. When we construct a thread, an instance of the `ThreadStart` or `ParameterizedThreadStart` delegate is passed to the constructor. The C# compiler is creating this object behind the scenes when we just type the name of the method we want to run in a different thread. Then we start a thread and run `PrintNumbers` in the usual manner on the main thread.

As a result, there will be two ranges of numbers from 1 to 10 randomly crossing each other. This illustrates that the `PrintNumbers` method runs simultaneously on the main thread and on the other thread.

Pausing a thread

This recipe will show you how to make a thread wait for some time without wasting operating system resources.

Getting ready

To work through this recipe, you will need Visual Studio 2012. There are no other prerequisites. The source code for this recipe can be found at `BookSamples\Chapter1\Recipe2`.

How to do it...

To understand how to make a thread wait without wasting operating system resource, perform the following steps:

1. Start Visual Studio 2012. Create a new C# **Console Application** project.

2. In the `Program.cs` file add the following `using` directives:

```
using System;
using System.Threading;
```

3. Add the following code snippet below the `Main` method:

```
static void PrintNumbers()
{
  Console.WriteLine("Starting...");
  for (int i = 1; i < 10; i++)
  {
    Console.WriteLine(i);
  }
}
static void PrintNumbersWithDelay()
{
  Console.WriteLine("Starting...");
  for (int i = 1; i < 10; i++)
  {
    Thread.Sleep(TimeSpan.FromSeconds(2));
    Console.WriteLine(i);
  }
}
```

4. Add the following code snippet inside the `Main` method:

```
Thread t = new Thread(PrintNumbersWithDelay);
t.Start();
PrintNumbers();
```

5. Run the program.

How it works...

When the program is run, it creates a thread that will execute a code in the `PrintNumbersWithDelay` method. Immediately after that, it runs the `PrintNumbers` method. The key feature here is adding the `Thread.Sleep` method call to a `PrintNumbersWithDelay` method. It causes a thread executing this code to wait a specified amount of time (two seconds in our case) before printing each number. While a thread is sleeping, it uses as little CPU time as possible. As a result, we will see that the code in the `PrintNumbers` method that usually runs later will be executed before the code in the `PrintNumbersWithDelay` method in a separate thread.

Making a thread wait

This recipe will show you how a program can wait for some computation in another thread to complete to use its result later in the code. It is not enough to use `Thread.Sleep` because we don't know the exact time the computation will take.

Getting ready

To work through this recipe, you will need Visual Studio 2012. There are no other prerequisites. The source code for this recipe can be found at `BookSamples\Chapter1\Recipe3`.

How to do it...

To understand how a program can wait for some computation in another thread to complete to use its result later, perform the following steps:

1. Start Visual Studio 2012. Create a new C# **Console Application** project.

2. In the `Program.cs` file, add the following `using` directives:

   ```
   using System;
   using System.Threading;
   ```

3. Add the following code snippet below the `Main` method:

   ```
   static void PrintNumbersWithDelay()
   {
     Console.WriteLine("Starting...");
     for (int i = 1; i < 10; i++)
     {
       Thread.Sleep(TimeSpan.FromSeconds(2));
       Console.WriteLine(i);
     }
   }
   ```

4. Add the following code snippet inside the `Main` method:

   ```
   Console.WriteLine("Starting...");
   Thread t = new Thread(PrintNumbersWithDelay);
   t.Start();
   t.Join();
   Console.WriteLine("Thread completed");
   ```

5. Run the program.

How it works...

When the program is run, it runs a long-running thread that prints out numbers and waits two seconds before printing each number. But in the main program, we called the `t.Join` method, which allows us to wait for thread `t` to complete. When it is complete, the main program continues to run. With the help of this technique, it is possible to synchronize execution steps between two threads. The first one waits until another one is complete and then continues to work. While the first thread is waiting, it is in a blocked state (as it is in the previous recipe when you call `Thread.Sleep`).

Aborting a thread

In this recipe, we will describe how to abort another thread's execution.

Getting ready

To work through this recipe, you will need Visual Studio 2012. There are no other prerequisites. The source code for this recipe can be found at `BookSamples\Chapter1\Recipe4`.

How to do it...

To understand how to abort another thread's execution, perform the following steps:

1. Start Visual Studio 2012. Create a new C# **Console Application** project.

2. In the `Program.cs` file, add the following `using` directives:

   ```
   using System;
   using System.Threading;
   ```

3. Add the following code snippet below the `Main` method:

   ```
   static void PrintNumbersWithDelay()
   {
     Console.WriteLine("Starting...");
     for (int i = 1; i < 10; i++)
     {
       Thread.Sleep(TimeSpan.FromSeconds(2));
       Console.WriteLine(i);
     }
   }
   ```

4. Add the following code snippet inside the `Main` method:

```
Console.WriteLine("Starting program...");
Thread t = new Thread(PrintNumbersWithDelay);
t.Start();
Thread.Sleep(TimeSpan.FromSeconds(6));
t.Abort();
Console.WriteLine("A thread has been aborted");
Thread t = new Thread(PrintNumbers);
t.Start();
PrintNumbers();
```

5. Run the program.

How it works...

When the main program and a separate number-printing thread run, we wait for 6 seconds and then call a `t.Abort` method on a thread. This injects a `ThreadAbortException` method into a thread causing it to terminate. It is very dangerous, generally because this exception can happen at any point and may totally destroy the application. In addition, it is not always possible to terminate a thread with this technique. The target thread may refuse to abort by handling this exception and calling the `Thread.ResetAbort` method. Thus, it is not recommended that you use the `Abort` method to close a thread. There are different methods that are preferred, such as providing a `CancellationToken` method to cancel a thread execution. This approach will be described in *Chapter 3*, *Using a Thread Pool*.

Determining a thread state

This recipe will describe possible states a thread could have. It is useful to get information about whether a thread is started yet or whether it is in a blocked state. Please note that because a thread runs independently, its state could be changed at any time.

Getting ready

To work through this recipe, you will need Visual Studio 2012. There are no other prerequisites. The source code for this recipe can be found at `BookSamples\Chapter1\Recipe5`.

How to do it...

To understand how to determine a thread state and acquire useful information about it, perform the following steps:

1. Start Visual Studio 2012. Create a new C# **Console Application** project.

2. In the `Program.cs` file, add the following `using` directives:

   ```csharp
   using System;
   using System.Threading;
   ```

3. Add the following code snippet below the `Main` method:

   ```csharp
   static void DoNothing()
   {
     Thread.Sleep(TimeSpan.FromSeconds(2));
   }

   static void PrintNumbersWithStatus()
   {
     Console.WriteLine("Starting...");
     Console.WriteLine(Thread.CurrentThread
     .ThreadState.ToString());
     for (int i = 1; i < 10; i++)
     {
       Thread.Sleep(TimeSpan.FromSeconds(2));
       Console.WriteLine(i);
     }
   }
   ```

4. Add the following code snippet inside the `Main` method:

   ```csharp
   Console.WriteLine("Starting program...");
   Thread t = new Thread(PrintNumbersWithStatus);
   Thread t2 = new Thread(DoNothing);
   Console.WriteLine(t.ThreadState.ToString());
   t2.Start();
   t.Start();
   for (int i = 1; i < 30; i++)
   {
     Console.WriteLine(t.ThreadState.ToString());
   }
   Thread.Sleep(TimeSpan.FromSeconds(6));
   t.Abort();
   Console.WriteLine("A thread has been aborted");
   Console.WriteLine(t.ThreadState.ToString());
   Console.WriteLine(t2.ThreadState.ToString());
   ```

5. Run the program.

How it works...

When the main program starts it defines two different threads; one of them will be aborted and the other runs successfully. The thread state is located in the `ThreadState` property of a `Thread` object, which is a C# enumeration. At first the thread has a `ThreadState.Unstarted` state. Then we run it and assume that, for the duration of 30 iterations of a cycle, the thread will change its state from `ThreadState.Running` to `ThreadState.WaitSleepJoin`.

> Please note that the current `Thread` object is always accessible through the `Thread.CurrentThread` static property.

If it does not happen, just increase the number of iterations. Then we abort the first thread and see that now it has a `ThreadState.Aborted` state. It is also possible that the program will print out the `ThreadState.AbortRequested` state. This illustrates very well the complexity of synchronizing two threads. Please keep in mind that you should not use thread abortion in your programs. I've covered it here only to show the corresponding thread state.

Finally, we can see that our second thread `t2` completed successfully and now has a `ThreadState.Stopped` state. There are several other states, but they are partly deprecated and partly not as useful as those we examined.

Thread priority

This recipe will describe the different possible options for thread priority. Setting a thread priority determines how much CPU time a thread will be given.

Getting ready

To work through this recipe, you will need Visual Studio 2012. There are no other prerequisites. The source code for this recipe can be found at `BookSamples\Chapter1\Recipe6`.

How to do it...

To understand the workings of thread priority, perform the following steps:

1. Start Visual Studio 2012. Create a new C# **Console Application** project.
2. In the `Program.cs` file, add the following `using` directives:

```
using System;
using System.Diagnostics;
using System.Threading;
```

3. Add the following code snippet below the `Main` method:

```
static void RunThreads()
{
  var sample = new ThreadSample();

  var threadOne = new Thread(sample.CountNumbers);
  threadOne.Name = "ThreadOne";
  var threadTwo = new Thread(sample.CountNumbers);
  threadTwo.Name = "ThreadTwo";

  threadOne.Priority = ThreadPriority.Highest;
  threadTwo.Priority = ThreadPriority.Lowest;
  threadOne.Start();
  threadTwo.Start();

  Thread.Sleep(TimeSpan.FromSeconds(2));
  sample.Stop();
}
class ThreadSample
{
  private bool _isStopped = false;
  public void Stop()
  {
    _isStopped = true;
  }

  public void CountNumbers()
  {
    long counter = 0;

    while (!_isStopped)
    {
      counter++;
    }

    Console.WriteLine("{0} with {1,11} priority " +
      "has a count = {2,13}",
      Thread.CurrentThread.Name,
      Thread.CurrentThread.Priority,
      counter.ToString("N0"));
  }
}
```

4. Add the following code snippet inside the `Main` method:

```
Console.WriteLine("Current thread priority: {0}",
  Thread.CurrentThread.Priority);
Console.WriteLine("Running on all cores available");
RunThreads();
Thread.Sleep(TimeSpan.FromSeconds(2));
Console.WriteLine("Running on a single core");
Process.GetCurrentProcess().ProcessorAffinity = new
  IntPtr(1);
RunThreads();
```

5. Run the program.

How it works...

When the main program starts, it defines two different threads. The first one, `ThreadPriority.Highest`, will have the highest thread priority, while the second one, that is `ThreadPriority.Lowest`, will have the lowest. We print out the main thread priority value and then start these two threads on all available cores. If we have more than one computing core, we should get an initial result within two seconds. The highest priority thread should calculate more iterations usually, but both values should be close. However, if there are any other programs running that load all the CPU cores, the situation could be quite different.

To simulate this situation, we set up the `ProcessorAffinity` option, instructing the operating system to run all our threads on a single CPU core (number one). Now the results should be very different and the calculations will take more than 2 seconds. This happens because the CPU core will run mostly the high-priority thread, giving the rest of the threads very little time.

Please note that this is an illustration of how an operating system works with thread prioritization. Usually, you should not write programs relying on this behavior.

Foreground and background threads

This recipe will describe what foreground and background threads are and how setting this option affects the program's behavior.

Getting ready

To work through this recipe, you will need Visual Studio 2012. There are no other prerequisites. The source code for this recipe can be found at `BookSamples\Chapter1\Recipe7`.

How to do it...

To understand the effect of foreground and background threads on a program, perform the following:

1. Start Visual Studio 2012. Create a new C# **Console Application** project.

2. In the `Program.cs` file, add the following `using` directives:

   ```
   using System;
   using System.Threading;
   ```

3. Add the following code snippet below the `Main` method:

   ```
   class ThreadSample
   {
     private readonly int _iterations;

     public ThreadSample(int iterations)
     {
       _iterations = iterations;
     }
     public void CountNumbers()
     {
       for (int i = 0; i < _iterations; i++)
       {
         Thread.Sleep(TimeSpan.FromSeconds(0.5));
         Console.WriteLine("{0} prints {1}",
           Thread.CurrentThread.Name, i);
       }
     }
   }
   ```

4. Add the following code snippet inside the `Main` method:

   ```
   var sampleForeground = new ThreadSample(10);
   var sampleBackground = new ThreadSample(20);

   var threadOne = new Thread(sampleForeground.CountNumbers);
   threadOne.Name = "ForegroundThread";
   var threadTwo = new Thread(sampleBackground.CountNumbers);
   threadTwo.Name = "BackgroundThread";
   threadTwo.IsBackground = true;

   threadOne.Start();
   threadTwo.Start();
   ```

5. Run the program.

How it works...

When the main program starts it defines two different threads. By default, a thread we create explicitly is a foreground thread. To create a background thread, we manually set the `IsBackground` property of the `threadTwo` object to `true`. We configure these threads in a way that the first one will complete faster, and then we run the program.

After the first thread completes, the program shuts down and the background thread terminates. This is the main difference between the two: a process waits for all the foreground threads to complete before finishing the work, but if it has background threads, they just shut down.

It is also important to mention that if a program defines a foreground thread that does not complete, the main program will not end properly.

Passing parameters to a thread

This recipe will describe how to provide a code we run in another thread with the required data. We will go through the different ways to fulfill this task and review common mistakes.

Getting ready

To work through this recipe, you will need Visual Studio 2012. There are no other prerequisites. The source code for this recipe can be found at `BookSamples\Chapter1\Recipe8`.

How to do it...

To understand how to pass parameters to a thread, perform the following steps:

1. Start Visual Studio 2012. Create a new C# **Console Application** project.

2. In the `Program.cs` file, add the following `using` directives:

   ```
   using System;
   using System.Threading;
   ```

3. Add the following code snippet below the `Main` method:

   ```
   static void Count(object iterations)
   {
     CountNumbers((int)iterations);
   }

   static void CountNumbers(int iterations)
   {
     for (int i = 1; i <= iterations; i++)
     {
   ```

```
      Thread.Sleep(TimeSpan.FromSeconds(0.5));
      Console.WriteLine("{0} prints {1}",
        Thread.CurrentThread.Name, i);
  }
}
static void PrintNumber(int number)
{
  Console.WriteLine(number);
}

class ThreadSample
{
  private readonly int _iterations;

  public ThreadSample(int iterations)
  {
    _iterations = iterations;
  }
  public void CountNumbers()
  {
    for (int i = 1; i <= _iterations; i++)
    {
      Thread.Sleep(TimeSpan.FromSeconds(0.5));
      Console.WriteLine("{0} prints {1}",
        Thread.CurrentThread.Name, i);
    }
  }
}
```

4. Add the following code snippet inside the `Main` method:

```
var sample = new ThreadSample(10);

var threadOne = new Thread(sample.CountNumbers);
threadOne.Name = "ThreadOne";
threadOne.Start();
threadOne.Join();
Console.WriteLine("--------------------------");

var threadTwo = new Thread(Count);
threadTwo.Name = "ThreadTwo";
threadTwo.Start(8);
threadTwo.Join();
Console.WriteLine("--------------------------");
```

```
var threadThree = new Thread(() => CountNumbers(12));
threadThree.Name = "ThreadThree";
threadThree.Start();
threadThree.Join();
Console.WriteLine("-------------------------");

int i = 10;
var threadFour = new Thread(() => PrintNumber(i));
i = 20;
var threadFive = new Thread(() => PrintNumber(i));
threadFour.Start();
threadFive.Start();
```

5. Run the program.

How it works...

When the main program starts, it first creates an object of class `ThreadSample`, providing it with a number of iterations. Then we start a thread with the object's method `CountNumbers`. This method runs in another thread, but it uses the number 10, which is the value that we passed to the object's constructor. Therefore, we just passed this number of iterations to another thread in the same indirect way.

There's more...

Another way to pass data is to use the `Thread.Start` method by accepting an object that can be passed to another thread. To work this way, a method that we started in another thread must accept one single parameter of type object. This option is illustrated by creating a `threadTwo` thread. We pass 8 as an object to the `Count` method, where it is cast to an `integer` type.

The next option involves using lambda expressions. A lambda expression defines a method that does not belong to any class. We create such a method that invokes another method with the arguments needed and start it in another thread. When we start the `threadThree` thread, it prints out 12 numbers, which are exactly the numbers we passed to it via the lambda expression.

Using the lambda expressions involves another C# construct named `closure`. When we use any local variable in a lambda expression, C# generates a class and makes this variable a property of this class. So actually, we do the same thing as in the `threadOne` thread, but we do not define the class ourselves; the C# compiler does this automatically.

This could lead to several problems; for example, if we use the same variable from several lambdas, they will actually share this variable value. This is illustrated by the previous example; when we start `threadFour` and `threadFive`, they will both print 20 because the variable was changed to hold the value 20 before both threads were started.

Locking with a C# lock keyword

This recipe will describe how to ensure that if one thread uses some resource, another does not simultaneously use it. We will see why this is needed and what the thread safety concept is all about.

Getting ready

To work through this recipe, you will need Visual Studio 2012. There are no other prerequisites The source code for this recipe can be found at `BookSamples\Chapter1\Recipe9`.

How to do it...

To understand how to use the C# lock keyword, perform the following steps:

1. Start Visual Studio 2012. Create a new C# **Console Application** project.

2. In the `Program.cs` file, add the following `using` directives:

    ```
    using System;
    using System.Threading;
    ```

3. Add the following code snippet below the `Main` method:

    ```
    static void TestCounter(CounterBase c)
    {
      for (int i = 0; i < 100000; i++)
      {
        c.Increment();
        c.Decrement();
      }
    }

    class Counter : CounterBase
    {
      public int Count { get; private set; }
      public override void Increment()
      {
        Count++;
      }

      public override void Decrement()
      {
        Count--;
      }
    }

    class CounterWithLock : CounterBase
    {
    ```

```
    private readonly object _syncRoot = new Object();

    public int Count { get; private set; }

    public override void Increment()
    {
      lock (_syncRoot)
      {
        Count++;
      }
    }

    public override void Decrement()
    {
      lock (_syncRoot)
      {
        Count--;
      }
    }
  }

  abstract class CounterBase
  {
    public abstract void Increment();
    public abstract void Decrement();
  }
```

4. Add the following code snippet inside the `Main` method:

```
Console.WriteLine("Incorrect counter");

var c = new Counter();

var t1 = new Thread(() => TestCounter(c));
var t2 = new Thread(() => TestCounter(c));
var t3 = new Thread(() => TestCounter(c));
t1.Start();
t2.Start();
t3.Start();
t1.Join();
t2.Join();
t3.Join();

Console.WriteLine("Total count: {0}",c.Count);
Console.WriteLine("-------------------------");
Console.WriteLine("Correct counter");
```

```
var c1 = new CounterWithLock();

t1 = new Thread(() => TestCounter(c1));
t2 = new Thread(() => TestCounter(c1));
t3 = new Thread(() => TestCounter(c1));
t1.Start();
t2.Start();
t3.Start();
t1.Join();
t2.Join();
t3.Join();
Console.WriteLine("Total count: {0}", c1.Count);
```

5. Run the program.

How it works...

When the main program starts, it first creates an object of the class `Counter`. This class defines a simple counter that can be incremented and decremented. Then we start three threads that share the same counter instance and perform an increment and decrement in a cycle. This leads to nondeterministic results. If we run the program several times, it will print out several different counter values. It could be zero, but mostly won't be.

This happens because the `Counter` class is not thread safe. When several threads access the counter at the same time, the first thread gets the counter value 10 and increments it to 11. Then a second thread gets the value 11 and increments it to 12. The first thread gets the counter value 12, but before a decrement happens, a second thread gets the counter value 12 as well. Then the first thread decrements 12 to 11 and saves it into the counter, and the second thread simultaneously does the same. As a result, we have two increments and only one decrement, which is obviously not right. This kind of a situation is called race condition and is a very common cause of errors in a multithreaded environment.

To make sure that this does not happen, we must ensure that while one thread works with the counter, all other threads must wait until the first one finishes the work. We can use the `lock` keyword to achieve this kind of behavior. If we `lock` an object, all the other threads that require an access to this object will be waiting in a blocked state until it is unlocked. This could be a serious performance issue and later, in *Chapter 2, Thread Synchronization*, we will learn more about this.

Locking with a Monitor construct

This recipe illustrates another common multithreaded error called a deadlock. Since a deadlock will cause a program to stop working, the first piece in this example is a new `Monitor` construct that allows us to avoid a deadlock. Then, the previously described `lock` keyword is used to get a deadlock.

Getting ready

To work through this recipe, you will need Visual Studio 2012. There are no other prerequisites. The source code for this recipe can be found at `BookSamples\ Chapter1\Recipe10`.

How to do it...

To understand the multithreaded error deadlock, perform the following steps:

1. Start Visual Studio 2012. Create a new C# **Console Application** project.

2. In the `Program.cs` file, add the following `using` directives:

   ```
   using System;
   using System.Threading;
   ```

3. Add the following code snippet below the `Main` method:

   ```
   static void LockTooMuch(object lock1, object lock2)
   {
     lock (lock1)
     {
       Thread.Sleep(1000);
       lock (lock2);
     }
   }
   ```

4. Add the following code snippet inside the `Main` method:

   ```
   object lock1 = new object();
   object lock2 = new object();

   new Thread(() => LockTooMuch(lock1, lock2)).Start();

   lock (lock2)
   {
   ```

```
    Thread.Sleep(1000);
    Console.WriteLine("Monitor.TryEnter allows not to get
        stuck, returning false after a specified timeout is
        elapsed");
    if (Monitor.TryEnter(lock1, TimeSpan.FromSeconds(5)))
    {
        Console.WriteLine("Acquired a protected resource
            succesfully");
    }
    else
    {
        Console.WriteLine("Timeout acquiring a resource!");
    }
}
new Thread(() => LockTooMuch(lock1, lock2)).Start();

Console.WriteLine("---------------------------------");
lock (lock2)
{
    Console.WriteLine("This will be a deadlock!");
    Thread.Sleep(1000);
    lock (lock1)
    {
        Console.WriteLine("Acquired a protected resource
            succesfully");
    }
}
```

5. Run the program.

How it works...

Let's start with the LockTooMuch method. In this method, we just lock the first object, wait a second and then lock the second object. Then we start this method in another thread and try to lock the second object and then the first object from the main thread.

If we use the lock keyword like in the second part of this demo, it would be a deadlock. The first thread holds a lock on the lock1 object and waits while the lock2 object gets free; the main thread holds a lock on the lock2 object and waits for the lock1 object to become free, which in this situation will never happen.

Actually, the `lock` keyword is a syntactic sugar for `Monitor` class usage. If we were to disassemble a code with `lock`, we would see that it turns into the following code snippet:

```
bool acquiredLock = false;
try
{
  Monitor.Enter(lockObject, ref acquiredLock);

  // Code that accesses resources that are protected by the lock.

}
finally
{
  if (acquiredLock)
  {
    Monitor.Exit(lockObject);
  }
}
```

Therefore, we can use the `Monitor` class directly; it has the `TryEnter` method, which accepts a timeout parameter and returns `false` if this timeout parameter expires before we can acquire the resource protected by `lock`.

Handling exceptions

This recipe will describe how to handle exceptions in other threads properly. It is very important to always place a `try/catch` block inside the thread because it is not possible to catch an exception outside a thread's code.

Getting ready

To work through this recipe, you will need Visual Studio 2012. There are no other prerequisites. The source code for this recipe can be found at `BookSamples\Chapter1\Recipe11`.

How to do it...

To understand the handling of exceptions in other threads, perform the following steps:

1. Start Visual Studio 2012. Create a new C# **Console Application** project.

2. In the `Program.cs` file add the following `using` directives:

```
using System;
using System.Threading;
```

3. Add the following code snippet below the `Main` method:

```
static void BadFaultyThread()
{
  Console.WriteLine("Starting a faulty thread...");
  Thread.Sleep(TimeSpan.FromSeconds(2));
  throw new Exception("Boom!");
}

static void FaultyThread()
{
  try
  {
    Console.WriteLine("Starting a faulty thread...");
    Thread.Sleep(TimeSpan.FromSeconds(1));
    throw new Exception("Boom!");
  }
  catch (Exception ex)
  {
    Console.WriteLine("Exception handled: {0}",
      ex.Message);
  }
}
```

4. Add the following code snippet inside the `Main` method:

```
var t = new Thread(FaultyThread);
t.Start();
t.Join();

try
{
  t = new Thread(BadFaultyThread);
  t.Start();
}
catch (Exception ex)
{
  Console.WriteLine("We won't get here!");
}
```

5. Run the program.

How it works...

When the main program starts, it defines two threads that will throw an exception. One of these threads handles exception, while the other does not. You can see that the second exception is not caught by a `try/catch` block around a code that starts the thread. So if you work with threads directly, the general rule is to not throw an exception from a thread, but to use a `try/catch` block inside a thread code instead.

In the older versions of .NET Framework (1.0 and 1.1), this behavior was different and uncaught exceptions did not force an application shutdown. It is possible to use this policy by adding an application configuration file (such as `app.config`) containing the following code snippet:

```
<configuration>
  <runtime>
    <legacyUnhandledExceptionPolicy enabled="1" />
  </runtime>
</configuration>
```

2

Thread Synchronization

In this chapter, we will describe some of the common techniques of working with shared resources from multiple threads. You will learn about:

- ▶ Performing basic atomic operations
- ▶ Using the Mutex construct
- ▶ Using the SemaphoreSlim construct
- ▶ Using the AutoResetEvent construct
- ▶ Using the ManualResetEventSlim construct
- ▶ Using the CountDownEvent construct
- ▶ Using the Barrier construct
- ▶ Using the ReaderWriterLockSlim construct
- ▶ Using the SpinWait construct

Introduction

As we saw in *Chapter 1, Threading Basics*, it is problematic to use a shared object simultaneously from several threads. It is very important to synchronize those threads so that they perform operations on that shared object in a proper sequence. In a multithreaded counter recipe, we met a problem called the race condition. It happened because the execution of those multiple threads were not synchronized properly. When one thread performs the increment and decrement operations, the other threads must wait for their turn. This general problem is often referred to as **thread synchronization**.

There are several ways to achieve thread synchronization. First, if there is no shared object, there is no need for synchronization at all. Surprisingly, it is very often that we can get rid of complex synchronization constructs by just redesigning your program and removing a shared state. If it's possible, just avoid using a single object from several threads.

If we must have a shared state, the second approach is to use only **atomic** operations. This means that an operation takes a single quantum of time and completes at once, so no other thread can perform another operation until the first operation is complete. Therefore, there is no need to make other threads wait for this operation to complete and there is no need to use locks; this in turn excludes the situation of a deadlock.

If this is not possible and the program's logic is more complicated, then we have to use different constructs to coordinate threads. One group of those constructs puts a waiting thread into a **blocked** state. In a blocked state, a thread uses as little CPU time as possible. However, this means that it will include at least one so-called **context switch**—the thread scheduler of an operating system—that will save the waiting thread's state, and switch to another thread, restoring its state by turn. This takes a considerable amount of resources; however, if the thread is going to be suspended for a long time, it is good. These kinds of constructs are also called **kernel-mode** constructs because only the kernel of an operating system is able to stop a thread from using CPU time.

In case we have to wait for a short period of time, it is better to simply wait than switch the thread to a blocked state. This will save us the context switch at the cost of some CPU time wasted while the thread is waiting. Such constructs are referred to as **user-mode** constructs. They are very lightweight and fast, but they waste a lot of CPU time in case a thread has to wait for long.

To use the best of both the worlds, there are **hybrid** constructs; these try to use the user-mode waiting first, and then if a thread waits long enough, it switches to a blocked state, saving CPU resources.

In this chapter, we will look through the aspects of thread synchronization. We will cover how to perform atomic operations and how to use the existing synchronization constructs included in the .NET framework.

Performing basic atomic operations

This recipe will show you how to perform basic atomic operations on an object to prevent the race condition without blocking threads.

Getting ready

To step through this recipe, you will need Visual Studio 2012. There are no other prerequisites. The source code for this recipe could be found at `7644_Code\Chapter2\Recipe1`.

How to do it...

To understand the basic atomic operations, perform the following steps:

1. Start Visual Studio 2012. Create a new C# **Console Application** project.

2. In the `Program.cs` file, add the following `using` directives:

```
using System;
using System.Threading;
```

3. Below the `Main` method, add the following code snippet:

```
static void TestCounter(CounterBase c)
{
  for (int i = 0; i < 100000; i++)
  {
    c.Increment();
    c.Decrement();
  }
}

class Counter : CounterBase
{
  private int _count;
  public int Count { get { return _count; } }

  public override void Increment()
  {
    _count++;
  }
}
```

```
    public override void Decrement()
    {
      _count--;
    }
}

class CounterNoLock : CounterBase
{
  private int _count;

  public int Count { get { return _count; } }

  public override void Increment()
  {
    Interlocked.Increment(ref _count);
  }

  public override void Decrement()
  {
    Interlocked.Decrement(ref _count);
  }
}

abstract class CounterBase
{
  public abstract void Increment();

  public abstract void Decrement();
}
```

4. Inside the `Main` method, add the following code snippet:

```
Console.WriteLine("Incorrect counter");

var c = new Counter();

var t1 = new Thread(() => TestCounter(c));
var t2 = new Thread(() => TestCounter(c));
var t3 = new Thread(() => TestCounter(c));
t1.Start();
t2.Start();
t3.Start();
t1.Join();
t2.Join();
t3.Join();
```

```
Console.WriteLine("Total count: {0}", c.Count);
Console.WriteLine("------------------------");
Console.WriteLine("Correct counter");

var c1 = new CounterNoLock();

t1 = new Thread(() => TestCounter(c1));
t2 = new Thread(() => TestCounter(c1));
t3 = new Thread(() => TestCounter(c1));
t1.Start();
t2.Start();
t3.Start();
t1.Join();
t2.Join();
t3.Join();
Console.WriteLine("Total count: {0}", c1.Count);
```

5. Run the program.

How it works...

When the program runs, it creates three threads that will execute a code in the `TestCounter` method. This method runs a sequence of increment/decrement operations on an object. Initially, the `Counter` object is not thread-safe and we get a race condition here. So in the first case, a counter value is not deterministic. We could get a zero value; however, if you run the program several times, you will eventually get some incorrect nonzero result.

In *Chapter 1, Threading Basics*, we resolved this problem by locking our object, causing other threads to block while one thread gets the old counter value, then computes and assigns a new value to the counter. However, if we execute this operation in such a way, it cannot be stopped midway; we would achieve the proper result without any locking with the help of the `Interlocked` construct. It provides the atomic methods `Increment`, `Decrement`, and `Add` for basic math, and it helps us to write the `Counter` class without the use of locking.

Using the Mutex construct

This recipe will describe how to synchronize two separate programs using a `Mutex` construct. `Mutex` is a primitive synchronization that grants exclusive access of the shared resource to only one thread.

Getting ready

To step through this recipe, you will need Visual Studio 2012. There are no other prerequisites. The source code for this recipe could be found at `7644_Code\Chapter2\Recipe2`.

How to do it...

To understand the synchronization of two separate programs using the `Mutex` construct, perform the following steps:

1. Start Visual Studio 2012. Create a new C# **Console Application** project.

2. In the `Program.cs` file, add the following `using` directives:
    ```
    using System;
    using System.Threading;
    ```

3. Inside the `Main` method, add the following code snippet:
    ```
    const string MutexName = "CSharpThreadingCookbook";

    using (var m = new Mutex(false, MutexName))
    {
      if (!m.WaitOne(TimeSpan.FromSeconds(5), false))
      {
        Console.WriteLine("Second instance is running!");
      }
      else
      {
        Console.WriteLine("Running!");
        Console.ReadLine();
        m.ReleaseMutex();
      }
    }
    ```

4. Run the program.

How it works...

When the main program starts, it defines a mutex with a specific name, providing the `initialOwner` flag as `false`. This allows the program to acquire a mutex if it is already created. Then, if no mutex was acquired, the program simply displays **Running**, and waits for any key to be pressed to release the mutex and exit.

If we start a second copy of the program, it will wait for 5 seconds, trying to acquire the mutex. If we press any key in the first copy of a program, the second one will start executing. However, if we keep waiting for 5 seconds, the second copy of the program will fail to acquire the mutex.

 Please note that a named mutex is a global operating system object! Always close the mutex properly; the best choice is to wrap a mutex object using a block.

This makes it possible to synchronize threads in different programs, which could be useful in a large number of scenarios.

Using the SemaphoreSlim construct

This recipe will show how to `SemaphoreSlim` is a lightweight version of `Semaphore`; it limits the number of threads that can access a resource concurrently.

Getting ready

To step through this recipe, you will need Visual Studio 2012. There are no other prerequisites. The source code for this recipe could be found at `BookSamples\Chapter2\Recipe3`.

How to do it...

To understand limiting a multithreaded access to a resource with the help of the `SemaphoreSlim` construct, perform the following steps:

1. Start Visual Studio 2012. Create a new C# **Console Application** project.

2. In the `Program.cs` file add the following `using` directives:

```
using System;
using System.Threading;
```

3. Below the `Main` method, add the following code snippet:

```
static SemaphoreSlim _semaphore = new SemaphoreSlim(4);


static void AccessDatabase(string name, int seconds)
{
  Console.WriteLine("{0} waits to access a database", name);
  _semaphore.Wait();
  Console.WriteLine("{0} was granted an access to a database",
    name);
  Thread.Sleep(TimeSpan.FromSeconds(seconds));
  Console.WriteLine("{0} is completed", name);
  _semaphore.Release();

}
```

4. Inside the `Main` method, add the following code snippet:

```
for (int i = 1; i <= 6; i++)
{
  string threadName = "Thread " + i;
  int secondsToWait = 2 + 2*i;
  var t = new Thread(() => AccessDatabase(threadName,
    secondsToWait));
  t.Start();
}
```

5. Run the program.

How it works...

When the main program starts, it creates a `SemaphoreSlim` instance, specifying the number of concurrent threads allowed in its constructor. Then it starts six threads with different names and start times to run.

Every thread is trying to acquire an access to a database, but we restrict the number of concurrent accesses to a database by four threads with the help of a semaphore. When four threads get an access to a database, the other two threads wait until one of the previous threads finishes its work and signals by calling the `_semaphore.Release` method.

There's more...

Here we use a hybrid construct, which allows us to save a context switch in cases where the wait time is less. However, there is an older version of this construct called `Semaphore`. This version is a pure, kernel-time construct. There is no sense in using it, except in one very important scenario; we can create a named semaphore like a named mutex and use it to synchronize threads in different programs. `SemaphoreSlim` does not use Windows kernel semaphores and does not support interprocess synchronization, so use `Semaphore` in this case.

Using the AutoResetEvent construct

In this recipe, there is an example of how to send notifications from one thread to another with the help of an `AutoResetEvent` construct. `AutoResetEvent` notifies a waiting thread that an event has occurred.

Getting ready

To step through this recipe, you will need Visual Studio 2012. There are no other prerequisites. The source code for this recipe could be found at `7644_Code\Chapter2\Recipe4`.

How to do it...

To understand how to send notifications from one thread to another with the help of the `AutoResetEvent` construct, perform the following steps:

1. Start Visual Studio 2012. Create a new C# **Console Application** project.

2. In the `Program.cs` file add the following `using` directives:

   ```
   using System;
   using System.Threading;
   ```

3. Below the `Main` method, add the following code snippet:

   ```
   private static AutoResetEvent _workerEvent = new
     AutoResetEvent(false);
   private static AutoResetEvent _mainEvent = new
     AutoResetEvent(false);

   static void Process(int seconds)
   {
     Console.WriteLine("Starting a long running work...");
     Thread.Sleep(TimeSpan.FromSeconds(seconds));
     Console.WriteLine("Work is done!");
     _workerEvent.Set();
     Console.WriteLine("Waiting for a main thread to complete
       its work");
     _mainEvent.WaitOne();
     Console.WriteLine("Starting second operation...");
     Thread.Sleep(TimeSpan.FromSeconds(seconds));
     Console.WriteLine("Work is done!");
     _workerEvent.Set();
   }
   ```

4. Inside the `Main` method, add the following code snippet:

   ```
   var t = new Thread(() => Process(10));
   t.Start();

   Console.WriteLine("Waiting for another thread to complete
     work");
   _workerEvent.WaitOne();
   Console.WriteLine("First operation is completed!");
   Console.WriteLine("Performing an operation on a main
     thread");
   Thread.Sleep(TimeSpan.FromSeconds(5));
   _mainEvent.Set();
   Console.WriteLine("Now running the second operation on a
     second thread");
   _workerEvent.WaitOne();
   Console.WriteLine("Second operation is completed!");
   ```

5. Run the program.

How it works...

When the main program starts, it defines two `AutoResetEvent` instances. One of them is for signaling from the second thread to the main thread, and the second one will be signaling from the main thread to the second thread. We provide `false` to the `AutoResetEvent` constructor, specifying the initial sate of both the instances as `unsignaled`. This means that any thread calling the `WaitOne` method of one of these objects will be blocked until we call the `Set` method. If we initialize the event state to `true`, it becomes `signaled` and the thirst thread calling `WaitOne` would proceed immediately. The event state then becomes `unsignaled` automatically, so we need to call the `Set` method once again to let the other threads calling the `WaitOne` method on this instance to continue.

Then we create a second thread, which will execute the first operation for 10 seconds and wait for the signal from the second thread. The signal means that the first operation is completed. Now the second thread is waiting for a signal from the main thread. We do some additional work on the main thread and send a signal by calling the `_mainEvent.Set` method. Then we wait for another signal from the second thread.

`AutoResetEvent` is a kernel-time construct, so if the wait time is not significant, it is better to use the next recipe with `ManualResetEventslim`, which is a hybrid construct.

Using the ManualResetEventSlim construct

This recipe will describe how to make signaling between threads more flexible with the `ManualResetEventSlim` construct.

Getting ready

To step through this recipe, you will need Visual Studio 2012. There are no other prerequisites. The source code for this recipe could be found at `BookSamples\Chapter2\Recipe5`.

How to do it...

To understand the use of the `ManualResetEventSlim` construct, perform the following steps:

1. Start Visual Studio 2012. Create a new C# **Console Application** project.
2. In the `Program.cs` file, add the following `using` directives:
   ```
   using System;
   using System.Threading;
   ```

3. Below the `Main` method, add the following code:

```
static ManualResetEventSlim _mainEvent = new
ManualResetEventSlim(false);

static void TravelThroughGates(string threadName,
  int seconds)
{
  Console.WriteLine("{0} falls to sleep", threadName);
  Thread.Sleep(TimeSpan.FromSeconds(seconds));
  Console.WriteLine("{0} waits for the gates to open!",
    threadName);
  _mainEvent.Wait();
  Console.WriteLine("{0} enters the gates!", threadName);
}
```

4. Inside the `Main` method, add the following code:

```
var t1 = new Thread(() => TravelThroughGates("Thread 1",
  5));
var t2 = new Thread(() => TravelThroughGates("Thread 2",
  6));
var t3 = new Thread(() => TravelThroughGates("Thread 3",
  12));
t1.Start();
t2.Start();
t3.Start();
Thread.Sleep(TimeSpan.FromSeconds(6));
Console.WriteLine("The gates are now open!");
_mainEvent.Set();
Thread.Sleep(TimeSpan.FromSeconds(2));
_mainEvent.Reset();
Console.WriteLine("The gates have been closed!");
Thread.Sleep(TimeSpan.FromSeconds(10));
Console.WriteLine("The gates are now open for the second
  time!");
_mainEvent.Set();
Thread.Sleep(TimeSpan.FromSeconds(2));
Console.WriteLine("The gates have been closed!");
_mainEvent.Reset();
```

5. Run the program.

How it works...

When the main program starts, it first creates an instance of the `ManualResetEventSlim` construct. Then we start three threads that will wait for this event to signal them to continue the execution.

The whole process of working with this construct is like letting people pass through a gate. The `AutoResetEvent` event that we looked at in the previous recipe works like a turnstile, allowing only one person to pass at a time. `ManualResetEventSlim`, which is a hybrid version of `ManualResetEvent`, stays open until we manually call the `Reset` method. Going back to the code, when we call `_mainEvent.Set`, we open it and allow the threads that are ready to accept this signal and continue working. However, thread number three is still sleeping and does not make it in time. We call `_mainEvent.Reset` and we thus close it. The last thread is now ready to go on, but it has to wait for the next signal, which will happen a few seconds later.

There's more...

As in one of the previous recipes, we use a hybrid construct that lacks the possibility to work at the operating system level. If we need to have a global event, we should use the `EventWaitHandle` construct, which is the base class for `AutoResetEvent` and `ManualResetEvent`.

Using the CountDownEvent construct

This recipe will describe how to use a `CountdownEvent` signaling construct to wait until a certain number of operations complete.

Getting ready

To step through this recipe, you will need Visual Studio 2012. There are no other prerequisites. The source code for this recipe could be found at `BookSamples\Chapter2\Recipe6`.

How to do it...

To understand the use of the `CountDownEvent` construct, perform the following steps:

1. Start Visual Studio 2012. Create a new C# **Console Application** project.

2. In the `Program.cs` file, add the following `using` directives:

   ```
   using System;
   using System.Threading;
   ```

3. Below the `Main` method, add the following code:

```
static CountdownEvent _countdown = new CountdownEvent(2);

static void PerformOperation(string message, int seconds)
{
  Thread.Sleep(TimeSpan.FromSeconds(seconds));
  Console.WriteLine(message);
  _countdown.Signal();
}
```

4. Inside the `Main` method, add the following code:

```
Console.WriteLine("Starting two operations");
var t1 = new Thread(() => PerformOperation("Operation 1 is
  completed", 4));
var t2 = new Thread(() => PerformOperation("Operation 2 is
  completed", 8));
t1.Start();
t2.Start();
_countdown.Wait();
Console.WriteLine("Both operations have been completed.");
_countdown.Dispose();
```

5. Run the program.

How it works...

When the main program starts, we create a new `CountdownEvent` instance, specifying that we want it to signal when two operations complete in its constructor. Then we start two threads that signal to the event when they complete. As soon as the second thread is complete, the main thread returns from waiting on `CountdownEvent` and proceeds further. Using this construct, it is very convenient to wait for multiple asynchronous operations to complete.

However, there is a significant disadvantage; `_countdown.Wait()` will wait forever if we fail to call `_countdown.Signal()` the required number of times. Please make sure that all your threads complete with the `Signal` method call when using `CountdownEvent`.

Using the Barrier construct

This recipe illustrates another interesting synchronization construct called `Barrier`. The `Barrier` construct helps to organize several threads to meet at some point in time, providing a callback that will be executed each time the threads have called the `SignalAndWait` method.

Getting ready

To step through this recipe, you will need Visual Studio 2012. There are no other prerequisites. The source code for this recipe could be found at `BookSamples\Chapter2\Recipe7`.

How to do it...

To understand the use of the `Barrier` construct, perform the following steps:

1. Start Visual Studio 2012. Create a new C# **Console Application** project.

2. In the `Program.cs` file, add the following `using` directives:

```
using System;
using System.Threading;
```

3. Below the `Main` method, add the following code:

```
static Barrier _barrier = new Barrier(2,
  b => Console.WriteLine("End of phase {0}",
    b.CurrentPhaseNumber + 1));

static void PlayMusic(string name, string message,
  int seconds)
{
  for (int i = 1; i < 3; i++)
  {
    Console.WriteLine("-------------------------------------
      ----------");
    Thread.Sleep(TimeSpan.FromSeconds(seconds));
    Console.WriteLine("{0} starts to {1}", name, message);
    Thread.Sleep(TimeSpan.FromSeconds(seconds));
    Console.WriteLine("{0} finishes to {1}", name,
      message);
    _barrier.SignalAndWait();
  }
}
```

4. Inside the `Main` method, add the following code:

```
var t1 = new Thread(() => PlayMusic("the guitarist",
  "play an amazing solo", 5));
var t2 = new Thread(() => PlayMusic("the singer",
  "sing his song", 2));

t1.Start();
t2.Start();
```

5. Run the program.

How it works...

We create a `Barrier` construct, specifying that we want to synchronize two threads, and after each of those two threads have called the `_barrier.SignalAndWait` method, we need to execute a callback that will print out the number of phases completed.

Each thread is going to send a signal to `Barrier` twice, so we will have two phases. Every time both the threads call the `SignalAndWait` method, `Barrier` will execute the callback. It is useful for working with multithreaded iteration algorithms, to execute some calculations on each iteration end. The end of iteration is reached when the last thread calls the `SignalAndWait` method.

Using the ReaderWriterLockSlim construct

This recipe will describe how to create a thread-safe mechanism to read and write to a collection from multiple threads using a `ReaderWriterLockSlim` construct. `ReaderWriterLockSlim` represents a lock that is used to manage access to a resource, allowing multiple threads for reading or exclusive access for writing.

Getting ready

To step through this recipe, you will need Visual Studio 2012. There are no other prerequisites. The source code for this recipe could be found at `BookSamples\Chapter2\Recipe8`.

How to do it...

To understand how to create a thread-safe mechanism to read and write to a collection from multiple threads using the `ReaderWriterLockSlim` construct, perform the following steps:

1. Start Visual Studio 2012. Create a new C# **Console Application** project.

2. In the `Program.cs` file, add the following `using` directives:

    ```
    using System;
    using System.Collections.Generic;
    using System.Threading;
    ```

3. Below the `Main` method, add the following code:

    ```
    static ReaderWriterLockSlim _rw = new
      ReaderWriterLockSlim();
    static Dictionary<int, int> _items =
      new Dictionary<int, int>();

    static void Read()
    ```

```
    {
      Console.WriteLine("Reading contents of a dictionary");
      while (true)
      {
        try
        {
          _rw.EnterReadLock();
          foreach (var key in _items.Keys)
          {
            Thread.Sleep(TimeSpan.FromSeconds(0.1));
          }
        }
        finally
        {
          _rw.ExitReadLock();
        }
      }
    }

    static void Write(string threadName)
    {
      while (true)
      {
        try
        {
          int newKey = new Random().Next(250);
          _rw.EnterUpgradeableReadLock();
          if (!_items.ContainsKey(newKey))
          {
            try
            {
              _rw.EnterWriteLock();
              _items[newKey] = 1;
              Console.WriteLine("New key {0} is added to a
                dictionary by a {1}", newKey, threadName);
            }
            finally
            {
              _rw.ExitWriteLock();
            }
          }
          Thread.Sleep(TimeSpan.FromSeconds(0.1));
        }
        finally
        {
          _rw.ExitUpgradeableReadLock();
        }
      }
    }
```

4. Inside the `Main` method, add the following code:

```
new Thread(Read){ IsBackground = true }.Start();
new Thread(Read){ IsBackground = true }.Start();
new Thread(Read){ IsBackground = true }.Start();

new Thread(() => Write("Thread 1")){ IsBackground =
    true }.Start();
new Thread(() => Write("Thread 2")){ IsBackground =
    true }.Start();

Thread.Sleep(TimeSpan.FromSeconds(30));
```

5. Run the program.

How it works...

When the main program starts, it simultaneously runs three threads that read data from a dictionary and two threads that write some data into this dictionary. To achieve thread safety, we use the `ReaderWriterLockSlim` construct, which was designed especially for such scenarios.

It has two kinds of locks: a read lock that allows multiple threads reading and a write lock that blocks every operation from other threads until this write lock is released. There is also an interesting scenario when we obtain a read lock, read some data from the collection, and depending on that data, decide to obtain a write lock and change the collection. If we get the write locks at once, too much time is spent not allowing our readers to read the data, because the collection is blocked when we get a write lock. To minimize this time, there are `EnterUpgradeableReadLock`/`ExitUpgradeableReadLock` methods. We get a read lock and read the data; if we find that we have to change the underlying collection, we just upgrade our lock using the `EnterWriteLock` method, then perform a write operation quickly, and release a write lock using `ExitWriteLock`.

In our case, we get a random number; we then get a read lock and check if this number exists in the dictionary keys collection. If not, we upgrade our lock to a write lock and then add this new key to a dictionary. It is a good practice to use `try/finally` blocks to make sure we always release locks after acquiring them.

All our threads have been created as background threads and after waiting for 30 seconds, the main thread as well as all the background threads complete.

Using the SpinWait construct

This recipe will describe how to wait on a thread without involving kernel-mode constructs. In addition, we introduce `SpinWait`, a hybrid synchronization construct, which is designed to wait in user mode for some time, and then switch to the kernel mode to save CPU time.

Getting ready

To step through this recipe, you will need Visual Studio 2012. There are no other prerequisites. The source code for this recipe could be found at `BookSamples\Chapter2\Recipe9`.

How to do it...

To understand waiting on a thread without involving kernel-mode constructs, perform the following steps:

1. Start Visual Studio 2012. Create a new C# **Console Application** project.

2. In the `Program.cs` file, add the following `using` directives:

```
using System;
using System.Threading;
```

3. Below the `Main` method, add the following code:

```
static volatile bool _isCompleted = false;

static void UserModeWait()
{
  while (!_isCompleted)
  {
    Console.Write(".");
  }
  Console.WriteLine();
  Console.WriteLine("Waiting is complete");
}

static void HybridSpinWait()
{
  var w = new SpinWait();
  while (!_isCompleted)
  {
    w.SpinOnce();
    Console.WriteLine(w.NextSpinWillYield);
  }
  Console.WriteLine("Waiting is complete");
}
```

4. Inside the `Main` method, add the following code:

```
var t1 = new Thread(UserModeWait);
var t2 = new Thread(HybridSpinWait);

Console.WriteLine("Running user mode waiting");
t1.Start();
Thread.Sleep(20);
_isCompleted = true;
Thread.Sleep(TimeSpan.FromSeconds(1));
_isCompleted = false;
Console.WriteLine("Running hybrid SpinWait construct
  waiting");
t2.Start();
Thread.Sleep(5);
_isCompleted = true;
```

5. Run the program.

How it works...

When the main program starts, it defines a thread that will execute an endless loop for 20 milliseconds until the main thread sets the `_isCompleted` variable to `true`. We could experiment and run this cycle for 20-30 seconds instead, measuring the CPU load with the Windows task manager. It will show a significant amount of processor time, depending on how many cores the CPU has.

We use the `volatile` keyword to declare the `_isCompleted` static field. The `volatile` keyword indicates that a field might be modified by multiple threads executing at the same time. Fields that are declared `volatile` are not subject to compiler and processor optimizations that assume access by a single thread. This ensures that the most up-to-date value is present in the field at all times.

Then we use a `SpinWait` version, which on each iteration prints a special flag that shows us whether a thread is going to switch to a blocked state. We run this thread for 5 milliseconds to see that. In the beginning, `SpinWait` tries to stay in user mode, and after about nine iterations, it begins to switch the thread to a blocked state. If we try to measure the CPU load with this version, we will not see any CPU usage in the Windows task manager.

3

Using a Thread Pool

In this chapter, we will describe common techniques for working with shared resources from multiple threads. You will learn about:

- ▶ Invoking a delegate on a thread pool
- ▶ Posting an asynchronous operation on a thread pool
- ▶ Thread pool and the degree of parallelism
- ▶ Implementing a cancellation option
- ▶ Using a wait handle and a timeout with a thread pool
- ▶ Using a timer
- ▶ Using the BackgroundWorker component

Introduction

In the previous chapters, we discussed several ways to create threads and organize their cooperation. Now let's consider another scenario where we create many asynchronous operations that take very little time to complete. As we discussed in the *Introduction* section of *Chapter 1, Threading Basics*, creating a thread is an expensive operation, so doing this for each short-lived, asynchronous operation will include a significant overhead expense.

To deal with this problem, there is a common approach called **pooling** that can be successfully applied to any situation when we need many short-lived, expensive resources. We allocate a certain amount of those resources in advance, and organize them into a resource pool. Each time we need a new resource, we just take it from the pool, instead of creating a new one, and return it to the pool after the resource is no longer needed.

The **.NET thread pool** is an implementation of this concept. It is accessible via the `System.Threading.ThreadPool` type. A thread pool is managed by .NET **Common Language Runtime** (**CLR**), which means that there is one instance of a thread pool per CLR. The `ThreadPool` type has a `QueueUserWorkItem` static method that accepts a **delegate**, representing a user-defined, asynchronous operation. After this method is called, this delegate goes to the internal queue. Then, if there are no threads inside the pool, it creates a new **worker thread** and puts the first delegate in the queue on it.

If we put new operations on a thread pool, after the previous operations are completed, it is possible to re-use this one thread to execute these operations. However, if we put new operations faster, the thread pool will create more threads to serve these operations. There is a limit to prevent creating too many threads, and in that case, new operations will wait in the queue until the worker threads in the pool become free to serve them.

> It is very important to keep operations on a thread pool short-lived! Do not put long-running operations on a thread pool or block worker threads. This will lead to all worker threads becoming busy, and they would no longer be able to serve user operations. This, in turn, will lead to performance problems and errors that are very hard to debug.

When we stop putting new operations on a thread pool, it will eventually remove threads that are no longer needed after being idle for some time. This will free up any operating system resources that are no longer required.

I would like to emphasize once again that a thread pool is intended to execute short-running operations. Using a thread pool gives us the possibility to save operating system resources at the cost of reducing the degree of parallelism. We use fewer threads, but execute asynchronous operations slower than usual, batching them by a number of worker threads available. This makes sense if operations are fast to complete, but it will degrade the performance for executing many long-running, compute-bound operations.

Another important thing to be very careful of is using a thread pool in ASP.NET applications. ASP.NET infrastructure uses a thread pool itself, and if you waste all worker threads from a thread pool, a web server will no longer be able to serve incoming requests. It is recommended to use only input/output bound asynchronous operations in ASP.NET, because they use a different mechanics called **I/O threads**. We will discuss I/O threads in *Chapter 9, Using asynchronous I/O*.

Please note that worker threads of a thread pool are background threads. This means that when all of the threads in the foreground (including the main application thread) are complete, then all the background threads will be stopped.

In this chapter, we will learn to use a thread pool to execute asynchronous operations. We will cover different ways to put an operation on a thread pool, and how to cancel an operation and prevent it from running for a long time.

Invoking a delegate on a thread pool

This recipe will show you how to execute a delegate asynchronously on a thread pool. In addition, we will discuss an approach called **Asynchronous Programming Model (APM)**, which was historically the first asynchronous programming pattern in .NET.

Getting ready

To step into this recipe, you will need Visual Studio 2012. There are no other prerequisites. The source code for this recipe could be found in `BookSamples\Chapter3\Recipe1`

How to do it...

To understand how to invoke a delegate on a thread pool, perform the following steps:

1. Start Visual Studio 2012. Create a new C# **Console Application** project.

2. In the `Program.cs` file, add the following `using` directives:

```
using System;
using System.Threading;
```

3. Add the following code snippet below the `Main` method:

```
private delegate string RunOnThreadPool(out int threadId);

private static void Callback(IAsyncResultar)
{
  Console.WriteLine("Starting a callback...");
  Console.WriteLine("State passed to a callback: {0}",
    ar.AsyncState);
  Console.WriteLine("Is thread pool thread: {0}",
    Thread.CurrentThread.IsThreadPoolThread);
  Console.WriteLine("Thread pool worker thread id: {0}",
    Thread.CurrentThread.ManagedThreadId);
}
```

```csharp
private static string Test(out intthreadId)
{
  Console.WriteLine("Starting...");
  Console.WriteLine("Is thread pool thread: {0}",
    Thread.CurrentThread.IsThreadPoolThread);
  Thread.Sleep(TimeSpan.FromSeconds(2));
  threadId = Thread.CurrentThread.ManagedThreadId;
  return string.Format("Thread pool worker thread id was:
    {0}", threadId);
}
```

4. Add the following code inside the `Main` method:

```csharp
int threadId = 0;

RunOnThreadPool poolDelegate = Test;

var t = new Thread(() => Test(out threadId));
t.Start();
t.Join();

Console.WriteLine("Thread id: {0}", threadId);

IAsyncResult r = poolDelegate.BeginInvoke(out threadId,
  Callback, "a delegate asynchronous call");
r.AsyncWaitHandle.WaitOne();

string result = poolDelegate.EndInvoke(out threadId, r);

Console.WriteLine("Thread pool worker thread id: {0}",
  threadId);
Console.WriteLine(result);

Thread.Sleep(TimeSpan.FromSeconds(2));
```

5. Run the program.

How it works...

When the program runs, it creates a thread in an old-fashioned way, and then starts it and waits for its completion. Since a thread constructor accepts only a method that does not return any result, we use a **lambda expression** to wrap up a call to the `Test` method. We make sure that this thread is not from the thread pool by printing out the `Thread.CurrentThread.IsThreadPoolThread` property value. We also print out a managed thread ID to identify a thread on which this code was executed.

Then we define a delegate and run it by calling the `BeginInvoke` method. This method accepts a callback that will be called after the asynchronous operation completes, and a user-defined state to pass into the callback. This state is usually used to distinguish one asynchronous call from another. As a result, we get a `result` object that implements the `IAsyncResult` interface. `BeginInvoke` returns the result immediately, allowing us to continue with any work while the asynchronous operation is being executed on a worker thread of the thread pool. When we need the result of an asynchronous operation, we use the `result` object returned from the `BeginInvoke` method call. We can poll on it using a result property `IsCompleted`, but in this case, we use the `AsyncWaitHandle` result property to wait on it until the operation is complete. After this is done, to get a result from it, we call the `EndInvoke` method on a delegate, passing the delegate arguments and our `IAsyncResult` object.

Actually, using `AsyncWaitHandle` is not necessary. If we comment out `r.AsyncWaitHandle.WaitOne`, the code will still run successfully, because the `EndInvoke` method actually waits for the asynchronous operation to complete. It is always important to call `EndInvoke` (or `EndOperationName` for other asynchronous APIs), because it throws any unhandled exceptions back to the calling thread. Always call both the `Begin` and `End` methods when using this kind of asynchronous API.

When the operation completes, a callback passed to the `BeginInvoke` method will be posted on a thread pool, more specifically, a worker thread. If we comment out the `Thread.Sleep` method call at the end of the `Main` method definition, the callback will not be executed. This is because when the main thread completes, all the background threads will be stopped, including this callback. It is possible that both asynchronous calls to a delegate and a callback will be served by the same worker thread, which is easy to see by a worker thread ID.

This approach of using the `BeginOperationName/EndOperationName` method and the `IAsyncResult` object in .NET is called Asynchronous Programming Model or the APM pattern, and such methods' pairs are called Asynchronous Methods. This pattern is still being used in various .NET class library APIs, but in modern programming, it is preferable to use **Task Parallel Library** (**TPL**) for organizing an asynchronous API. We will cover this topic in *Chapter 4, Using Task Parallel Library*.

Posting an asynchronous operation on a thread pool

This recipe will describe how to put an asynchronous operation on a thread pool.

Getting ready

To step into this recipe, you will need Visual Studio 2012. There are no other prerequisites. The source code for this recipe could be found in `BookSamples\Chapter3\Recipe2`.

How to do it...

To understand how to post an asynchronous operation on a thread pool, perform the following steps:

1. Start Visual Studio 2012. Create a new C# **Console Application** project.

2. In the `Program.cs` file, add the following `using` directives:

    ```
    using System;
    usingSystem.Threading;
    ```

3. Add the following code snippet below the `Main` method:

    ```
    private static void AsyncOperation(object state)
    {
      Console.WriteLine("Operation state: {0}",
        state ?? "(null)");
      Console.WriteLine("Worker thread id: {0}",
        Thread.CurrentThread.ManagedThreadId);
      Thread.Sleep(TimeSpan.FromSeconds(2));
    }
    ```

4. Add the following code snippet inside the `Main` method:

    ```
    const int x = 1;
    const int y = 2;
    const string lambdaState = "lambda state 2";

    ThreadPool.QueueUserWorkItem(AsyncOperation);
    Thread.Sleep(TimeSpan.FromSeconds(1));
    ```

```
ThreadPool.QueueUserWorkItem(AsyncOperation,
    "async state");
Thread.Sleep(TimeSpan.FromSeconds(1));

ThreadPool.QueueUserWorkItem( state => {
  Console.WriteLine("Operation state: {0}", state);
  Console.WriteLine("Worker thread id: {0}",
    Thread.CurrentThread.ManagedThreadId);
  Thread.Sleep(TimeSpan.FromSeconds(2));
}, "lambda state");

ThreadPool.QueueUserWorkItem( _ => {
  Console.WriteLine("Operation state: {0}, {1}", x+y,
    lambdaState);
  Console.WriteLine("Worker thread id: {0}",
    Thread.CurrentThread.ManagedThreadId);
  Thread.Sleep(TimeSpan.FromSeconds(2));
}, "lambda state");

Thread.Sleep(TimeSpan.FromSeconds(2));
```

5. Run the program.

How it works...

First, we define the `AsyncOperation` method that accepts a single parameter of the object type. Then, we post this method on a thread pool using the `QueueUserWorkItem` method. Then we post this method once again, but this time we pass a `state` object to this method call. This object will be passed to the `AsynchronousOperation` method as the `state` parameter.

Make a thread sleep for 1 second after those operations provide a thread pool with the possibility to re-use threads for new operations. If you comment these `Thread.Sleep` calls, most certainly, thread IDs will be different in all cases. If not, probably the first two threads will be re-used to run the following two operations.

First, we post a lambda expression to a thread pool. Nothing special here; instead of defining a separate method, we use the lambda expression syntax.

Secondly, instead of passing the state of a lambda expression, we use **closure** mechanics. It gives us more flexibility, and allows us to provide more than one object to the asynchronous operation and static typing for those objects. So the previous mechanism of passing an object into a method callback is really redundant and obsolete. There is no need to use it now when we have closures in C#.

Thread pool and the degree of parallelism

This recipe will show how a thread pool works with many asynchronous operations, and how it is different from creating many separate threads.

Getting ready

To step into this recipe, you will need Visual Studio 2012. There are no other prerequisites. The source code for this recipe could be found in `BookSamples\Chapter3\Recipe3`.

How to do it...

To learn how a thread pool works with many asynchronous operations and how it is different from creating many separate threads, perform the following steps:

1. Start Visual Studio 2012. Create a new C# **Console Application** project.

2. In the `Program.cs` file, add the following `using` directives:

```
using System;
using System.Diagnostics;
using System.Threading;
```

3. Add the following code snippet below the `Main` method:

```
static void UseThreads(int numberOfOperations)
{
  using (var countdown = new CountdownEvent(
    numberOfOperations)) {

    Console.WriteLine("Scheduling work by creating
      threads");
    for (int i=0; i<numberOfOperations; i++) {
      var thread = new Thread(() => {
        Console.Write("{0},", Thread.CurrentThread.
          ManagedThreadId);
        Thread.Sleep(TimeSpan.FromSeconds(0.1));
        countdown.Signal();
      });
      thread.Start();
    }
    countdown.Wait();
    Console.WriteLine();
  }
}
```

```
static void UseThreadPool(int numberOfOperations)
{
    using (var countdown = new CountdownEvent(
        numberOfOperations)) {

        Console.WriteLine("Starting work on a threadpool");
        for (int i=0; i<numberOfOperations; i++) {
            ThreadPool.QueueUserWorkItem( _ => {
                Console.Write("{0},", Thread.CurrentThread.
                    ManagedThreadId);
                Thread.Sleep(TimeSpan.FromSeconds(0.1));
                countdown.Signal();
            });
        }
        countdown.Wait();
        Console.WriteLine();
    }
}
```

4. Add the following code snippet inside the `Main` method:

```
const int numberOfOperations = 500;
var sw = new Stopwatch();
sw.Start();
UseThreads(numberOfOperations);
sw.Stop();
Console.WriteLine("Execution time using threads: {0}",
    sw.ElapsedMilliseconds);

sw.Reset();
sw.Start();
UseThreadPool(numberOfOperations);
sw.Stop();
Console.WriteLine("Execution time using threads: {0}",
    sw.ElapsedMilliseconds);
```

5. Run the program.

How it works...

When the main program starts, we create many different threads and run an operation on each one of them. This operation prints out a thread ID and blocks a thread for 100 milliseconds. As a result, we create 500 threads, which run all of those operations in parallel. The total time on my machine is about 300 milliseconds, but we consume many operating system resources for all those threads.

Then, we follow the same procedure, but instead of creating a thread for each operation, we post them on a thread pool. After this, the thread pool starts to serve these operations; it begins to create more threads near the end, but still, it takes much more time, about 12 seconds on my machine. We save memory and threads for an operating system usage but pay with an execution time for it.

Implementing a cancellation option

In this recipe, there is an example on how to cancel an asynchronous operation on a thread pool.

Getting ready

To step into this recipe, you will need Visual Studio 2012. There are no other prerequisites. The source code for this recipe could be found in `BookSamples\Chapter3\Recipe4`.

How to do it...

To understand how to implement a cancellation option on a thread, perform the following steps:

1. Start Visual Studio 2012. Create a new C# **Console Application** project.

2. In the `Program.cs` file, add the following `using` directives:

```
using System;
using System.Threading;
```

3. Add the following code snippet below the `Main` method:

```
static void AsyncOperation1(CancellationToken token) {
  Console.WriteLine("Starting the first task");
  for (int i=0; i<5; i++) {
    if (token.IsCancellationRequested) {
      Console.WriteLine("The first task has been
        canceled.");
      return;
    }
```

```
      Thread.Sleep(TimeSpan.FromSeconds(1));
    }
    Console.WriteLine("The first task has completed
      succesfully");
  }

  static void AsyncOperation2(CancellationToken token) {
    try {
      Console.WriteLine("Starting the second task");

      for (int i=0; i<5; i++) {
        token.ThrowIfCancellationRequested();
        Thread.Sleep(TimeSpan.FromSeconds(1));
      }
      Console.WriteLine("The second task has completed
        successfully");
    }
    catch (OperationCanceledException) {
      Console.WriteLine("The second task has been
        canceled.");
    }
  }

  private static void AsyncOperation3(
    CancellationToken token) {

    boolcancellationFlag = false;
    token.Register(()=>cancellationFlag=true);
    Console.WriteLine("Starting the third task");
    for (int i=0; i<5; i++) {
      if (cancellationFlag) {
        Console.WriteLine("The third task has been
          canceled.");
        return;
      }
      Thread.Sleep(TimeSpan.FromSeconds(1));
    }
    Console.WriteLine("The third task has completed
      succesfully");
  }
```

4. Add the following code snippet inside the `Main` method:

```
using (var cts = new CancellationTokenSource()) {
  CancellationToken token = cts.Token;
  ThreadPool.QueueUserWorkItem(_ => AsyncOperation1(
    token));
  Thread.Sleep(TimeSpan.FromSeconds(2));
  cts.Cancel();
}

using (var cts = new CancellationTokenSource()) {
  CancellationToken token = cts.Token;
  ThreadPool.QueueUserWorkItem(_ => AsyncOperation2(
    token));
  Thread.Sleep(TimeSpan.FromSeconds(2));
  cts.Cancel();
}

using (var cts = new CancellationTokenSource()) {
  CancellationToken token = cts.Token;
  ThreadPool.QueueUserWorkItem(_ => AsyncOperation3(
    token));
  Thread.Sleep(TimeSpan.FromSeconds(2));
  cts.Cancel();
}

Thread.Sleep(TimeSpan.FromSeconds(2));
```

5. Run the program.

How it works...

Here, we introduce new `CancellationTokenSource` and `CancellationToken` constructs. They appeared in .NET 4.0, and now are the de facto standard for implementing asynchronous operations' cancellation process. Since a thread pool has been existing for long time, it has no special API for cancellation tokens; however, they still could be used.

In this program, we see three ways to organize a cancellation process. The first is just to poll and check the `CancellationToken.IsCancellationRequested` property. If it is set to `true`, it means that our operation is being cancelled, and we must abandon the operation.

The second way is to throw an `OperationCancelledException` exception. This allows for controlling the cancellation process not from inside the operation, which is being cancelled, but from the code on the outside.

The last option is to register a **callback** that will be called on a thread pool when an operation is cancelled. This will allow chaining a cancellation logic into another asynchronous operation.

Using a wait handle and timeout with a thread pool

This recipe will describe how to implement a timeout for thread pool operations, and how to wait properly on a thread pool.

Getting ready

To step into this recipe, you will need Visual Studio 2012. There are no other prerequisites. The source code for this recipe could be found in `BookSamples\Chapter3\Recipe5`.

How to do it...

To learn how to implement a timeout and how to wait properly on a thread pool, perform the following steps:

1. Start Visual Studio 2012. Create a new C# **Console Application** project.

2. In the `Program.cs` file, add the following `using` directives:
    ```
    using System;
    using System.Threading;
    ```

3. Add the following code snippet below the `Main` method:
    ```
    static void RunOperations(TimeSpanworkerOperationTimeout) {
      using (var evt = new ManualResetEvent(false))
      using (var cts = new CancellationTokenSource()) {
        Console.WriteLine("Registering timeout operations...");
        var worker = ThreadPool.RegisterWaitForSingleObject(
          evt, (state, isTimedOut) => WorkerOperationWait(cts,
            isTimedOut), null, workerOperationTimeout, true);

        Console.WriteLine("Starting long running
          operation...");

        ThreadPool.QueueUserWorkItem(_ => WorkerOperation(cts.Token,
    evt));

        Thread.Sleep(workerOperationTimeout.Add(TimeSpan.
          FromSeconds(2)));
        worker.Unregister(evt);
      }
    }
    ```

```
static void WorkerOperation(CancellationToken token,
  ManualResetEventevt) {

  for(int i=0; i<6; i++) {
    if (token.IsCancellationRequested) {
      return;
    }
    Thread.Sleep(TimeSpan.FromSeconds(1));
  }
  evt.Set();
}

static void WorkerOperationWait(CancellationTokenSource cts
  bool isTimedOut) {

  if (isTimedOut) {
    cts.Cancel();
    Console.WriteLine("Worker operation timed out and was
      canceled.");
  }
  else {
    Console.WriteLine("Worker operation succeded.");
  }
}
```

4. Add the following code snippet inside the `Main` method:

```
RunOperations(TimeSpan.FromSeconds(5));
RunOperations(TimeSpan.FromSeconds(7));
```

5. Run the program.

How it works...

A thread pool has another useful method: `ThreadPool.RegisterWaitForSingleObject`. This method allows us to queue a callback on a thread pool, and this callback will be executed when the provided wait handle is signaled or a timeout has occurred. This allows us to implement a timeout for thread pool operations.

First, we queue a long-running operation on a thread pool. It runs for 6 seconds and then sets a `ManualResetEvent` signaling construct, in case it completes successfully. In other case, if cancellation is requested, the operation is just abandoned.

Then, we register the second asynchronous operation that will be called when it receives a signal from the `ManualResetEvent` object, which is set by the first operation if it is completed successfully. Another option is when a timeout has occurred before the first operation is completed. If this happens, we use `CancellationToken` to cancel the first operation.

Finally, if we provide a 5-second timeout for the operation, it would not be enough. This is because the operation takes 6 seconds to complete, and we'd need to cancel this operation. So if we provide a 7-second timeout, which is acceptable, the operation completes successfully.

There's more...

This is very useful when you have a large number of threads that must wait in the blocked state for some multithreaded event construct to signal. Instead of blocking all those threads, we are able to use the thread pool infrastructure. It will allow to free up these threads until the event is set. This is a very important scenario for server applications, which require scalability and performance.

Using a timer

This recipe will describe how to use a `System.Threading.Timer` object to create periodically-called asynchronous operations on a thread pool.

Getting ready

To step into this recipe, you will need Visual Studio 2012. There are no other prerequisites. The source code for this recipe could be found in `BookSamples\Chapter3\Recipe6`.

How to do it...

To learn how to create periodically-called asynchronous operations on a thread pool, perform the following steps:

1. Start Visual Studio 2012. Create a new C# **Console Application** project.

2. In the `Program.cs` file, add the following `using` directives:

   ```
   using System;
   using System.Threading;
   ```

3. Add the following code snippet below the `Main` method:

   ```
   static Timer _timer;

   static void TimerOperation(DateTime start) {
     TimeSpan elapsed = DateTime.Now - start;
     Console.WriteLine("{0} seconds from {1}. Timer thread
       pool thread id: {2}", elapsed.Seconds, start,
       Thread.CurrentThread.ManagedThreadId);
   }
   ```

4. Add the following code snippet inside the `Main` method:

```
Console.WriteLine("Press 'Enter' to stop the timer...");
DateTime start = DateTime.Now;
_timer = new Timer(_ => TimerOperation(start), null,
  TimeSpan.FromSeconds(1), TimeSpan.FromSeconds(2));

Thread.Sleep(TimeSpan.FromSeconds(6));

_timer.Change(TimeSpan.FromSeconds(1),
  TimeSpan.FromSeconds(4));

Console.ReadLine();

_timer.Dispose();
```

5. Run the program.

How it works...

First, we create a new `Timer` instance. The first parameter is a lambda expression that will be executed on a thread pool. We call the `TimerOperation` method providing it with a start date. We do not use the user `state` object, so the second parameter is null; then, we specify when are we going to run `TimerOperation` for the first time, and what will be the period between calls. So the first value actually means that we start the first operation in a second, and then we run each of them for 2 seconds.

After this, we wait for 6 seconds and change our timer. We start `TimerOperation` in a second after calling the `_timer.Change` method, and then run each of them for 4 seconds.

Timer could be more complex than this!

It is possible to use a timer in a more complicated way. For instance, we can run the timer operation only once, providing a timer period parameter with the `Timeout.Infinte` value. Then, inside the timer asynchronous operation, we are able to set the next time when the timer operation will be executed, depending on some custom logic.

Lastly, we wait for the *Enter* key to be pressed and finish the application. While it is running, we can see the time passed since the program started.

Using the BackgroundWorker component

This recipe describes another approach to asynchronous programming by example of a `BackgroundWorker` component. With the help of this object, we are able to organize our asynchronous code as a set of events and event handlers. You will learn how to use this component for asynchronous programming.

Getting ready

To step into this recipe, you will need Visual Studio 2012. There are no other prerequisites. The source code for this recipe could be found in `BookSamples\Chapter3\Recipe7`.

How to do it...

To learn how to use the `BackgroundWorker` component, perform the following steps:

1. Start Visual Studio 2012. Create a new C# **Console Application** project.

2. In the `Program.cs` file, add the following `using` directives:

```
using System;
using System.ComponentModel;
using System.Threading;
```

3. Add the following code snippet below the `Main` method:

```
static void Worker_DoWork(object sender, DoWorkEventArgs e)
{
  Console.WriteLine("DoWork thread pool thread id: {0}",
    Thread.CurrentThread.ManagedThreadId);
  var bw = (BackgroundWorker) sender;
  for (int i=1; i<=100; i++) {

    if (bw.CancellationPending) {
      e.Cancel = true;
      return;
    }

    if (i%10 == 0) {
      bw.ReportProgress(i);
    }

    Thread.Sleep(TimeSpan.FromSeconds(0.1));
  }
  e.Result = 42;
}
```

```csharp
    static void Worker_ProgressChanged(object sender,
      ProgressChangedEventArgs e){

      Console.WriteLine("{0}% completed. Progress thread pool
        thread id: {1}", e.ProgressPercentage, Thread.
          CurrentThread.ManagedThreadId);
    }

    static void Worker_Completed(object sender,
      RunWorkerCompletedEventArgs e) {

      Console.WriteLine("Completed thread pool thread id: {0}",
        Thread.CurrentThread.ManagedThreadId);
      if (e.Error != null) {
        Console.WriteLine("Exception {0} has occured.",
          e.Error.Message);
      }
      else if (e.Cancelled) {
        Console.WriteLine("Operation has been canceled.");
      }
      else {
        Console.WriteLine("The answer is: {0}", e.Result);
      }
    }
```

4. Add the following code snippet inside the `Main` method:

```csharp
var bw = new BackgroundWorker();
bw.WorkerReportsProgress = true;
bw.WorkerSupportsCancellation = true;

bw.DoWork += Worker_DoWork;
bw.ProgressChanged += Worker_ProgressChanged;
bw.RunWorkerCompleted += Worker_Completed;

bw.RunWorkerAsync();

Console.WriteLine("Press C to cancel work");
do {
  if (Console.ReadKey(true).KeyChar == 'C') {
    bw.CancelAsync();
  }

}
while(bw.IsBusy);
```

5. Run the program.

How it works...

When the program starts, we create an instance of a `BackgroundWorker` component. We explicitly state that we want our background-worker-supported operations' cancellation and notifications on the operation's progress.

Now, this is where the most interesting part comes into play. Instead of manipulating with a thread pool and delegates, we use another C# idiom called **events**. An event represents one *source* of some notification and a number of *subscribers* ready to react when a notification arrives. In our case, we state that we would subscribe for three events, and when they occur, we would call the corresponding **event handlers**. These are methods with a specially defined signature that will be called when an event notifies its subscribers.

Therefore, instead of organizing an asynchronous API in a pair of `Begin`/`End` methods, it is possible to just start an asynchronous operation and then subscribe to different events that could happen while this operation is being executed. This approach is called **Event-based Asynchronous Pattern** (**EAP**). It was historically the second attempt to structure asynchronous programs, and now it is recommended to use TPL, which will be described in *Chapter 4, Using Task Parallel Library*.

So, we have subscribed to three events. The first of them is the `DoWork` event. A handler of this event will be called when a background worker object starts an asynchronous operation with the `RunWorkerAsync` method. The event handler will be executed on a thread pool, and this is the main operating point where work is canceled if cancellation is requested, and where we provide information on the progress of the operation. At last, when we get the result, we set it to event arguments, and then the `RunWorkerCompleted` event handler is called. Inside this method, we find out whether our operation is succeeded, or maybe there were some errors, or it was canceled.

Besides that, a `BackgroundWorker` component is actually intended to be used in **Windows Forms Applications** (**WPF**). Its implementation makes working with UI controls possible from a background worker event handler's code directly, which is very comfortable as compared to the interaction of worker threads of a thread pool with UI controls.

4
Using Task Parallel Library

In this chapter, we will dive into a new asynchronous programming paradigm, Task Parallel Library. You will learn the following:

- ▶ Creating a task
- ▶ Performing basic operations with a task
- ▶ Combining tasks together
- ▶ Converting the APM pattern to tasks
- ▶ Converting the EAP pattern to tasks
- ▶ Implementing a cancellation option
- ▶ Handling exceptions in tasks
- ▶ Running tasks in parallel
- ▶ Tweaking tasks execution with TaskScheduler

Introduction

In the previous chapters, we learned what a thread is, how to use threads, and why we need a thread pool. Using a thread pool allows us to save operating system resources at the cost of reducing a parallelism degree. We can think of thread pool as an **abstraction layer** that hides details of thread usage from a programmer, allowing us to concentrate on a program's logic rather than on threading issues.

However, using a thread pool is complicated as well. There is no easy way to get a result from a thread pool worker thread. We need to implement our own way to get a result back, and in case of exception, we have to propagate it to the original thread properly. Besides this, there is no easy way to create a set of dependent asynchronous actions, where one action runs after another finishes its work.

There were several attempts to work around those issues, which resulted in the creation of Asynchronous Programming Model and Event-based Asynchronous Pattern, mentioned in *Chapter 3, Using a Thread Pool*. These patterns made getting results easier, and did a good work with propagating exceptions, but combining asynchronous actions together still required a lot of work and resulted in a large amount of code.

To resolve all these problems, a new API for asynchronous operations was introduced in .Net Framework 4.0. It is called **Task Parallel Library** (**TPL**). It was changed slightly in .Net Framework 4.5, and to make it clear, we will work with the latest version of TPL by using the 4.5 Version of .Net Framework in our projects. TPL can be considered as one more abstraction layer over a thread pool, hiding the lower-level code that will work with the thread pool from a programmer, and supplying a more convenient and fine-grained API.

The core concept of TPL is a task. A task represents an asynchronous operation, which can be run in a variety of ways, using a separate thread or not. We will look through all possibilities in detail in this chapter.

By default, a programmer is not aware how exactly the task is executing. TPL raises the level of abstraction by hiding the task implementation details from the user. Unfortunately, in some cases this could lead to mysterious errors, such as hanging the application while trying to get a result from the task. This chapter will help to understand mechanics under the hood of TPL, and how to avoid using it in improper ways.

A task can be combined with other tasks in different variations. For example, we are able to start several tasks simultaneously, wait for all of them to complete, and then run a task that will perform some calculations over all the previous tasks' results. Convenient APIs for task combination is one of the key advantages of TPL compared to the previous patterns.

There are also several ways to deal with exceptions resulting from tasks. Since a task may consist of several another tasks, and they in turn have their child tasks as well, there is a concept of `AggregateException`. This type of exception is holding all exceptions from underlying tasks inside, allowing handling them separately.

And, last but not least, C# 5.0 has built-in support for TPL, allowing us to work with tasks in a very smooth and comfortable way using the new `await` and `async` keywords. We will discuss this topic in *Chapter 5, Using C# 5.0*.

In this chapter, we will learn to use TPL to execute asynchronous operations. We will learn what a task is, cover different ways to create tasks, and how to combine tasks together. We will also discuss how to convert legacy APM and EAP patterns to use tasks, how to handle exceptions properly, how to cancel tasks, and how to work with several tasks executing simultaneously. In addition, we will find out how to deal with tasks in Windows GUI applications properly.

Creating a task

This recipe shows a basic concept of what a task is. You will learn how to create and execute tasks.

Getting ready

To step through this recipe, you will need **Visual Studio 2012**. There are no other prerequisites. The source code for this recipe could be found at BookSamples\Chapter4\Recipe1.

How to do it...

To create and execute a task, perform the following steps:

1. Start Visual Studio 2012. Create a new C# **Console Application** project.

 This time, please make sure that you are using .Net Framework 4.5. From now on, we will be using this version for every project.

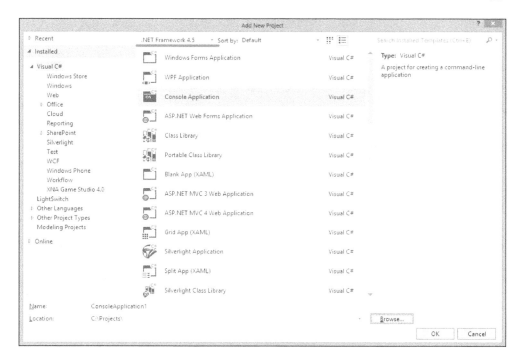

2. In the `Program.cs` file, add the following `using` directives:

    ```
    using System;
    using System.Threading;
    using System.Threading.Tasks;
    ```

3. Add the following code snippet below the `Main` method:

    ```
    static void TaskMethod(string name){
        Console.WriteLine("Task {0} is running on a thread id
            {1}. Is thread pool thread: {2}", name,
                Thread.CurrentThread.ManagedThreadId,
                    Thread.CurrentThread.IsThreadPoolThread);
    }
    ```

4. Add the following code snippet inside the `Main` method:

    ```
    var t1 = new Task(() =>TaskMethod("Task 1"));
    var t2 = new Task(() =>TaskMethod("Task 2"));
    t2.Start();
    t1.Start();
    Task.Run(() =>TaskMethod("Task 3"));
    Task.Factory.StartNew(() => TaskMethod("Task 4"));
    Task.Factory.StartNew(() => TaskMethod("Task 5"),
        TaskCreationOptions.LongRunning);
    Thread.Sleep(TimeSpan.FromSeconds(1));
    ```

5. Run the program.

How it works...

When the program runs, it creates two tasks with its constructor. We pass the lambda expression as the `Action` delegate; this allows us to provide a string parameter to `TaskMethod`. Then, we run these tasks by using the `Start` method.

> Please note that until we call the `Start` method on those tasks, they will not start executing. It is very easy to forget to actually start the task.

Then, we run two more tasks using the `Task.Run` and `Task.Factory.StartNew` methods. The difference is that both the created tasks immediately start working, so we do not need to call the `Start` method on the tasks explicitly. All of the tasks, number `Task 1` to `Task 4`, are placed on thread pool worker threads and run in an unspecified order. If you run the program several times, you will find that the tasks' execution order is not defined.

The `Task.Run` method is just a shortcut to `Task.Factory.StartNew`, but the latter method has additional options. In general, use the former method unless you need to do something special, as in case of `Task 5`. We mark this task as long running, and as a result, this task will be run on a separate thread not using a thread pool. However, this behavior could change, depending on the current **task scheduler** that runs the task. You will learn what a task scheduler is in the last recipe of this chapter.

Performing basic operations with a task

This recipe will describe how to get the result value from a task. We will go through. several scenarios to understand the difference between running a task on a thread pool or on a main thread.

Getting ready

To start this recipe, you will need Visual Studio 2012. There are no other prerequisites. The source code for this recipe could be found at `BookSamples\Chapter4\Recipe2`.

How to do it...

To perform basic operations with a task, perform the following steps:

1. Start Visual Studio 2012. Create a new C# **Console Application** project.

2. In the `Program.cs` file, add the following `using` directives:

    ```
    using System;
    using System.Threading;
    using System.Threading.Tasks;
    ```

3. Add the following code snippet below the `Main` method:

    ```
    static Task<int>CreateTask(string name){
      return new Task<int>(() =>TaskMethod(name));
    }

    static int TaskMethod(string name){
      Console.WriteLine("Task {0} is running on a thread id
        {1}. Is thread pool thread: {2}",name,
          Thread.CurrentThread.ManagedThreadId,
            Thread.CurrentThread.IsThreadPoolThread);
      Thread.Sleep(TimeSpan.FromSeconds(2));
      return 42;
    }
    ```

4. Add the following code snippet inside the `Main` method:

```
TaskMethod("Main Thread Task");
Task<int> task = CreateTask("Task 1");
task.Start();
int result = task.Result;
Console.WriteLine("Result is: {0}", result);

task = CreateTask("Task 2");
task.RunSynchronously();
result = task.Result;
Console.WriteLine("Result is: {0}", result);

task = CreateTask("Task 3");
task.Start();

while (!task.IsCompleted){
  Console.WriteLine(task.Status);
  Thread.Sleep(TimeSpan.FromSeconds(0.5));
}

Console.WriteLine(task.Status);
result = task.Result;
Console.WriteLine("Result is: {0}", result);
```

5. Run the program.

How it works...

At first, we run `TaskMethod` without wrapping it into a task. As a result, it is executing synchronously, providing us with the information about the main thread. Obviously, it is not a thread-pool thread.

Then we run `Task 1`, starting it with the `Start` method and waiting for the result. This task will be placed on a thread pool, and the main thread waits and is blocked until the task returns.

We do the same with `Task 2`, except that we run it using the `RunSynchronously()` method. This task will run on the main thread, and we get exactly the same output as in the very first case when we just called `TaskMethod` synchronously. This is a very useful optimization, allowing us to avoid thread pool usage for very short-lived operations.

We run `Task 3` in the same way we did with `Task 1`, but instead of blocking the main thread, we just spin, printing out the task status until the task is completed. This shows several task statuses, which are `Created`, `Running`, and `RanToCompletion` respectively.

Combining tasks together

This recipe will show how to set up tasks that are dependent on each other. We will learn how to create a task that will run after the parent task completes. In addition, we will discover a possibility to save thread usage for very short-lived tasks.

Getting ready

To step through this recipe, you will need Visual Studio 2012. There are no other prerequisites. The source code for this recipe can be found at `BookSamples\Chapter4\Recipe3`.

How to do it...

For combining tasks together, perform the following steps:

1. Start Visual Studio 2012. Create a new C# **Console Application** project.

2. In the `Program.cs` file, add the following `using` directives:

    ```
    using System;
    using System.Threading;
    using System.Threading.Tasks;
    ```

3. Add the following code snippet below the `Main` method:

    ```
    static int TaskMethod(string name, int seconds){
      Console.WriteLine("Task {0} is running on a thread id
        {1}. Is thread pool thread: {2}", name,
          Thread.CurrentThread.ManagedThreadId,
            Thread.CurrentThread.IsThreadPoolThread);
      Thread.Sleep(TimeSpan.FromSeconds(seconds));
      return 42 * seconds;
    }
    ```

4. Add the following code snippet inside the `Main` method:

    ```
    var firstTask = new Task<int>(() =>TaskMethod("First Task",
      3));
    var secondTask = new Task<int>(() =>TaskMethod("Second
      Task", 2));

    firstTask.ContinueWith(
      t =>Console.WriteLine("The first answer is {0}. Thread id
        {1}, is thread pool thread: {2}", t.Result,
          Thread.CurrentThread.ManagedThreadId,
            Thread.CurrentThread.IsThreadPoolThread),
              TaskContinuationOptions.OnlyOnRanToCompletion);
    ```

```
firstTask.Start();
secondTask.Start();

Thread.Sleep(TimeSpan.FromSeconds(4));

Task continuation = secondTask.ContinueWith(
  t =>Console.WriteLine("The second answer is {0}. Thread
    id {1}, is thread pool thread: {2}", t.Result,
      Thread.CurrentThread.ManagedThreadId,
        Thread.CurrentThread.IsThreadPoolThread),
          TaskContinuationOptions.OnlyOnRanToCompletion |
            TaskContinuationOptions.ExecuteSynchronously);

continuation.GetAwaiter().OnCompleted(
  () =>Console.WriteLine("Continuation Task Completed!
    Thread id {0}, is thread pool thread: {1}",
      Thread.CurrentThread.ManagedThreadId,
        Thread.CurrentThread.IsThreadPoolThread));

Thread.Sleep(TimeSpan.FromSeconds(2));
Console.WriteLine();

firstTask = new Task<int>(() => {
  varinnerTask = Task.Factory.StartNew(() =>TaskMethod(
    "Second Task", 5), TaskCreationOptions.
      AttachedToParent);
  innerTask.ContinueWith(t =>TaskMethod("Third Task", 2),
    TaskContinuationOptions.AttachedToParent);
  return TaskMethod("First Task", 2);
});

firstTask.Start();

while (!firstTask.IsCompleted){
  Console.WriteLine(firstTask.Status);
  Thread.Sleep(TimeSpan.FromSeconds(0.5));
}
Console.WriteLine(firstTask.Status);

Thread.Sleep(TimeSpan.FromSeconds(10));
```

5. Run the program.

How it works...

When the main program starts, we create two tasks, and for the first task we set up a **continuation** (a block of code that runs after the antecedent task is complete). Then we start both the tasks and wait for 4 seconds, which is enough for both tasks to complete. Then we run another continuation to the second task and try to execute it synchronously by specifying a `TaskContinuationOptions.ExecuteSynchronously` option. This is a useful technique when the continuation is very short-lived, and it will be faster to run it on the main thread than to put it on a thread pool. We are able to achieve this because the second task is completed by that moment. If we comment out the 4 seconds `Thread.Sleep` method, we will see that this code will be put on a thread pool because we do not have the result from the antecedent task yet.

Finally, we define a continuation for the previous continuation, but in a slightly different manner, using the new `GetAwaiter` and `OnCompleted` methods. These methods are intended to be used along with C# 5.0 language asynchronous mechanics. We will cover this topic later in *Chapter 5, Using C# 5.0*.

The last part of the demo is about the parent-child task relationships. We create a new task, and while running this task, we run a so-called child task by providing a `TaskCreationOptions.AttachedToParent` option.

 The child task must be created while running a parent task to attach to the parent properly!

This means that the parent task *will not complete* until all child tasks finish its work. We are also able to run continuations on a child tasks providing a `TaskContinuationOptions.AttachedToParent` option. This continuation will affect the parent task as well, and it will not complete until the very last child task ends.

Converting the APM pattern to tasks

In this recipe, we will see how to convert an old-fashioned APM API to a task. There are examples of different situations that could happen in the process of conversion.

Getting ready

To start this recipe, you will need Visual Studio 2012. There are no other prerequisites. The source code for this recipe can be found at `BookSamples\Chapter4\Recipe4`.

How to do it...

For converting the APM pattern to tasks, perform the following steps:

1. Start Visual Studio 2012. Create a new C# **Console Application** project.

2. In the `Program.cs` file, add the following `using` directives:

    ```
    using System;
    using System.Threading;
    using System.Threading.Tasks;
    ```

3. Add the following code snippet below the `Main` method:

    ```
    private delegate string AsynchronousTask(string
      threadName);
    private delegate string IncompatibleAsynchronousTask(out
      int threadId);

    private static void Callback(IAsyncResultar){
      Console.WriteLine("Starting a callback...");
      Console.WriteLine("State passed to a callback: {0}",
        ar.AsyncState);
      Console.WriteLine("Is thread pool thread: {0}",
        Thread.CurrentThread.IsThreadPoolThread);
      Console.WriteLine("Thread pool worker thread id: {0}",
        Thread.CurrentThread.ManagedThreadId);
    }

    private static string Test(string threadName){
      Console.WriteLine("Starting...");
      Console.WriteLine("Is thread pool thread: {0}",
        Thread.CurrentThread.IsThreadPoolThread);
      Thread.Sleep(TimeSpan.FromSeconds(2));
      Thread.CurrentThread.Name = threadName;
      return string.Format("Thread name: {0}",
        Thread.CurrentThread.Name);
    }

    private static string Test(out int threadId){
      Console.WriteLine("Starting...");
      Console.WriteLine("Is thread pool thread: {0}",
        Thread.CurrentThread.IsThreadPoolThread);
      Thread.Sleep(TimeSpan.FromSeconds(2));
      threadId = Thread.CurrentThread.ManagedThreadId;
      return string.Format("Thread pool worker thread id was:
        {0}", threadId);
    }
    ```

4. Add the following code snippet inside the `Main` method:

```
int threadId;
AsynchronousTask d = Test;
IncompatibleAsynchronousTask e = Test;

Console.WriteLine("Option 1");
Task<string> task = Task<string>.Factory.FromAsync(
  d.BeginInvoke("AsyncTaskThread", Callback, "a delegate
    asynchronous call"), d.EndInvoke);

task.ContinueWith(t =>Console.WriteLine("Callback is
  finished, now running a continuation! Result: {0}",
    t.Result));

while (!task.IsCompleted){
  Console.WriteLine(task.Status);
  Thread.Sleep(TimeSpan.FromSeconds(0.5));
}
Console.WriteLine(task.Status);
Thread.Sleep(TimeSpan.FromSeconds(1));

Console.WriteLine("-------------------------------------");
Console.WriteLine();
Console.WriteLine("Option 2");

task = Task<string>.Factory.FromAsync(
  d.BeginInvoke, d.EndInvoke, "AsyncTaskThread", "a
    delegate asynchronous call");
task.ContinueWith(t =>Console.WriteLine("Task is completed,
  now running a continuation! Result: {0}",
    t.Result));
while (!task.IsCompleted){
  Console.WriteLine(task.Status);
  Thread.Sleep(TimeSpan.FromSeconds(0.5));
}
Console.WriteLine(task.Status);
Thread.Sleep(TimeSpan.FromSeconds(1));

Console.WriteLine("-------------------------------------");
Console.WriteLine();
Console.WriteLine("Option 3");

IAsyncResult ar = e.BeginInvoke(out threadId, Callback, "a
  delegate asynchronous call");
ar = e.BeginInvoke(out threadId, Callback, "a delegate
  asynchronous call");
```

```
task = Task<string>.Factory.FromAsync(ar, _ =>e.EndInvoke(
    out threadId, ar));
task.ContinueWith(t =>
    Console.WriteLine("Task is completed, now running a
        continuation! Result: {0}, ThreadId: {1}",
            t.Result, threadId));

while (!task.IsCompleted){
    Console.WriteLine(task.Status);
    Thread.Sleep(TimeSpan.FromSeconds(0.5));
}
Console.WriteLine(task.Status);

Thread.Sleep(TimeSpan.FromSeconds(1));
```

5. Run the program.

How it works...

Here we define two kinds of delegates; one of them is using the `out` parameter and therefore is incompatible with the standard TPL API for converting the APM pattern to tasks. Then we have three examples of such a conversion.

The key point for converting APM to TPL is a `Task<T>.Factory.FromAsync` method, where `T` is the asynchronous operation result type. There are several overloads of this method; in the first case, we pass `IAsyncResult` and `Func<IAsyncResult, string>`, which is a method that accepts `IAsyncResult` implementation and returns a string. Since the first delegate type provides `EndMethod` that is compatible with this signature, we have no problem converting this delegate asynchronous call to a task.

In the second example, we do almost the same, but use a different `FromAsync` method overload, which does not allow specifying a callback that will be executed after the asynchronous delegate call completes. We are able to replace this with continuation, but if the callback is important, we can use the first example.

The last example shows a little trick. This time, `EndMethod` of the `IncompatibleAsynchronousTask` delegate uses the `out` parameter, and is not compatible with any `FromAsync` method overload. However, it is very easy to wrap the `EndMethod` call into a lambda expression that will be suitable for the task factory.

To see what is going on with the underlying task, we are printing its status while waiting for the asynchronous operation's result. We see that the first task's status is `WaitingForActivation`, which means that the task was not actually started yet by the TPL infrastructure.

Converting the EAP pattern to tasks

This recipe will describe how to translate event-based asynchronous operations to tasks. In this recipe, you will find a solid pattern that is suitable for every event-based asynchronous API in the .NET Framework class library.

Getting ready

To begin this recipe, you will need Visual Studio 2012. There are no other prerequisites. The source code for this recipe can be found at `BookSamples\Chapter4\Recipe5`.

How to do it...

For converting the EAP pattern to tasks, perform the following steps:

1. Start Visual Studio 2012. Create a new C# **Console Application** project.

2. In the `Program.cs` file, add the following `using` directives:

   ```
   using System;
   using System.ComponentModel;
   using System.Threading;
   using System.Threading.Tasks;
   ```

3. Add the following code snippet below the `Main` method:

   ```
   static int TaskMethod(string name, int seconds){
     Console.WriteLine("Task {0} is running on a thread id
       {1}. Is thread pool thread: {2}", name,
         Thread.CurrentThread.ManagedThreadId,
           Thread.CurrentThread.IsThreadPoolThread);
     Thread.Sleep(TimeSpan.FromSeconds(seconds));
     return 42 * seconds;
   }
   ```

4. Add the following code snippet inside the `Main` method:

   ```
   var tcs = new TaskCompletionSource<int>();

   var worker = new BackgroundWorker();
   worker.DoWork += (sender, eventArgs) =>
   {
     eventArgs.Result = TaskMethod("Background worker", 5);
   };
   ```

```
    worker.RunWorkerCompleted += (sender, eventArgs) =>{
      if (eventArgs.Error != null) {
        tcs.SetException(eventArgs.Error);
      }
      else if (eventArgs.Cancelled) {
        tcs.SetCanceled();
      }
        else {
          tcs.SetResult((int)eventArgs.Result);
        }
    };

    worker.RunWorkerAsync();

    int result = tcs.Task.Result;

    Console.WriteLine("Result is: {0}", result);
```

5. Run the program.

How it works...

This is a very simple and elegant example of converting EAP patterns to tasks. The key point is to use the `TaskCompletionSource<T>` type, where `T` is an asynchronous operation result type.

It is also important to not forget to wrap the `tcs.SetResult` method call into the `try-catch` block to guarantee that the error information is always set to the task completion source object. It is also possible to use the `TrySetResult` method instead of `SetResult` to make sure that the result has been set successfully.

Implementing a cancellation option

This recipe is about implementing the cancellation process for task-based asynchronous operations. We will learn how to use the cancellation token properly for tasks, and how to find out whether a task is cancelled before it was actually run.

Getting ready

To start with this recipe, you will need Visual Studio 2012. There are no other prerequisites. The source code for this recipe can be found at `BookSamples\Chapter4\Recipe6`.

How to do it...

For implementing a cancellation option for task-based asynchronous operations, perform the following steps:

1. Start Visual Studio 2012. Create a new C# **Console Application** project.

2. In the `Program.cs` file, add the following `using` directives:

```
using System;
using System.Threading;
using System.Threading.Tasks;
```

3. Add the following code snippet below the `Main` method:

```
private static int TaskMethod(string name, int seconds,
   CancellationToken token){

   Console.WriteLine("Task {0} is running on a thread id
     {1}. Is thread pool thread: {2}", name,
       Thread.CurrentThread.ManagedThreadId,
         Thread.CurrentThread.IsThreadPoolThread);
   for (int i = 0; i< seconds; i ++) {
     Thread.Sleep(TimeSpan.FromSeconds(1));
     if (token.IsCancellationRequested)
       return -1;
   }
   return 42*seconds;
}
```

4. Add the following code snippet inside the `Main` method:

```
var cts = new CancellationTokenSource();
var longTask = new Task<int>(() =>TaskMethod("Task 1", 10,
   cts.Token), cts.Token);
Console.WriteLine(longTask.Status);
cts.Cancel();
Console.WriteLine(longTask.Status);
Console.WriteLine("First task has been cancelled before
   execution");
cts = new CancellationTokenSource();
longTask = new Task<int>(() =>TaskMethod("Task 2", 10,
   cts.Token), cts.Token);
longTask.Start();
for (int i = 0; i< 5; i++ ){
   Thread.Sleep(TimeSpan.FromSeconds(0.5));
   Console.WriteLine(longTask.Status);
}
```

```
cts.Cancel();
for (int i = 0; i< 5; i++){
  Thread.Sleep(TimeSpan.FromSeconds(0.5));
  Console.WriteLine(longTask.Status);
}

Console.WriteLine("A task has been completed with result
  {0}.", longTask.Result);
```

5. Run the program.

How it works...

This is another very simple example of how to implement the cancellation option for a TPL task, as you are already familiar with the cancellation token concept we discussed in *Chapter 3, Using a Thread Pool*.

First, let's look closely at the `longTask` creation code. We'll pass a cancellation token to the underlying task once and then to the task constructor the second time. *Why do we need to supply this token twice?*

The answer is that if we cancel the task before it was actually started, its TPL infrastructure is responsible for dealing with the cancellation, because our code will not execute at all. We know that the first task was canceled by getting its status. If we will try to call the `Start` method on this task, we will get `InvalidOperationException`.

Then, we deal with the cancellation process from our own code. This means that we are now fully responsible for the cancellation process, and after we canceled the task, its status is still `RanToCompletion`, because from TPL's perspective, the task finished its job normally. It is very important to distinguish these two situations and understand the responsibility difference in each case.

Handling exceptions in tasks

This recipe describes the very important topic of handling exceptions in asynchronous tasks. We will go through different aspects of what happens to exceptions thrown from tasks and how to get to their information.

Getting ready

To step through this recipe, you will need Visual Studio 2012. There are no other prerequisites. The source code for this recipe can be found at `BookSamples\Chapter4\Recipe7`.

How to do it...

For handling exceptions in tasks, perform the following steps:

1. Start Visual Studio 2012. Create a new C# **Console Application** project.

2. In the `Program.cs` file, add the following `using` directives:

```
using System;
using System.Threading;
using System.Threading.Tasks;
```

3. Add the following code snippet below the `Main` method:

```
static int TaskMethod(string name, int seconds){
  Console.WriteLine("Task {0} is running on a thread id
    {1}. Is thread pool thread: {2}", name,
      Thread.CurrentThread.ManagedThreadId,
        Thread.CurrentThread.IsThreadPoolThread);
  Thread.Sleep(TimeSpan.FromSeconds(seconds));
  throw new Exception("Boom!");
  return 42 * seconds;
}
```

4. Add the following code snippet inside the `Main` method:

```
Task<int> task;
try{
  task = Task.Run(() =>TaskMethod("Task 1", 2));
  int result = task.Result;
  Console.WriteLine("Result: {0}", result);
}
catch (Exception ex){
  Console.WriteLine("Exception caught: {0}", ex);
}
Console.WriteLine("-----------------------------------------
------");
Console.WriteLine();

try{
  task = Task.Run(() =>TaskMethod("Task 2", 2));
  int result = task.GetAwaiter().GetResult();
  Console.WriteLine("Result: {0}", result);
}
catch (Exception ex){
  Console.WriteLine("Exception caught: {0}", ex);
}
```

```
Console.WriteLine("---------------------------------------
    ------");
Console.WriteLine();

var t1 = new Task<int>(() =>TaskMethod("Task 3", 3));
var t2 = new Task<int>(() =>TaskMethod("Task 4", 2));
var complexTask = Task.WhenAll(t1, t2);
var exceptionHandler = complexTask.ContinueWith(t =>
    Console.WriteLine("Exception caught: {0}", t.Exception),
      TaskContinuationOptions.OnlyOnFaulted);
t1.Start();
t2.Start();

Thread.Sleep(TimeSpan.FromSeconds(5));
```

5. Run the program.

How it works...

When the program starts, we create a task and try to get the task results synchronously. The Get part of the Result property makes the current thread wait until the completion of the task and propagates the exception to the current thread. In this case, we easily catch the exception in catch block, but this exception is a wrapper exception called AggregateException. In this case, it holds only one exception inside, because only one task has thrown this exception, and it is possible to get the underlying exception by accessing the InnerException property.

The second example is mostly the same, but to access the task result we use the GetAwaiter and GetResult methods. In this case, we do not have wrapper exception because it is unwrapped by the TPL infrastructure. We have an original exception at once, which is quite comfortable if we have only one underlying task.

The last example shows the situation where we have two task-throwing exceptions. To handle exceptions, we use now a continuation, which is executed only in case the antecedent task finishes with exception. This behavior is achieved by providing a TaskContinuationOptions.OnlyOnFaulted option to a continuation. As a result, we have AggregateException being printed out, and we have two inner exceptions from the both tasks inside it.

There's more...

As tasks may be connected in a very different manner, the resulting `AggregateException` exception might contain other aggregate exceptions inside along with the usual exceptions. Those inner aggregate exceptions might themselves contain other aggregate exceptions within them.

To get rid of those wrappers, we should use the root aggregate exception's `Flatten` method. It will return a collection of all the inner exceptions of every child aggregate exception in the hierarchy.

Running tasks in parallel

This recipe shows how to handle many asynchronous tasks running simultaneously. We will learn how to be notified effectively when all tasks are complete or any of the running tasks have to finish their work.

Getting ready

To start this recipe, you will need Visual Studio 2012. There are no other prerequisites. The source code for this recipe can be found at `BookSamples\Chapter4\Recipe8`.

How to do it...

For running tasks in parallel, perform the following steps:

1. Start Visual Studio 2012. Create a new C# **Console Application** project.

2. In the `Program.cs` file, add the following `using` directives:

```
using System;
using System.Collections.Generic;
using System.Threading;
using System.Threading.Tasks;
```

3. Add the following code snippet below the `Main` method:

```
static int TaskMethod(string name, int seconds){
  Console.WriteLine("Task {0} is running on a thread id
    {1}. Is thread pool thread: {2}", name,
      Thread.CurrentThread.ManagedThreadId,
        Thread.CurrentThread.IsThreadPoolThread);
  Thread.Sleep(TimeSpan.FromSeconds(seconds));
  return 42 * seconds;
}
```

4. Add the following code snippet inside the `Main` method:

```
var firstTask = new Task<int>(() =>TaskMethod("First Task",
  3));
var secondTask = new Task<int>(() =>TaskMethod("Second
  Task", 2));
var whenAllTask = Task.WhenAll(firstTask, secondTask);

whenAllTask.ContinueWith(t =>
  Console.WriteLine("The first answer is {0}, the second is
    {1}", t.Result[0], t.Result[1]),
      TaskContinuationOptions.OnlyOnRanToCompletion);

firstTask.Start();
secondTask.Start();

Thread.Sleep(TimeSpan.FromSeconds(4));

var tasks = new List<Task<int>>();
for (int i = 1; i< 4; i++)
{
  int counter = i;
  var task = new Task<int>(() =>TaskMethod(string.Format(
    "Task {0}", counter), counter));
  tasks.Add(task);
  task.Start();
}
```

```
while (tasks.Count> 0){
  var completedTask = Task.WhenAny(tasks).Result;
  tasks.Remove(completedTask);
  Console.WriteLine("A task has been completed with result
    {0}.", completedTask.Result);
}

Thread.Sleep(TimeSpan.FromSeconds(1));
```

5. Run the program.

How it works...

When the program starts, we create two tasks, and then with the help of the `Task.WhenAll` method, we create a third task, which will complete after all the tasks are complete. The resulting task provides us with an answers array, where the first element holds the first task's result, the second element holds the second result, and so on.

Then, we create another list of tasks and wait for any of those tasks to complete with the `Task.WhenAny` method. After we have one finished task, we remove it from the list and continue to wait for the other tasks to complete until the list is empty. This method is useful to get the tasks' completion progress or to use timeout while running the tasks. For example, we wait for a number of tasks and one of those tasks is counting a timeout. If this task completes first, we just cancel those tasks that are not completed yet.

Tweaking tasks execution with TaskScheduler

This recipe describes another very important aspect of dealing with tasks, which is a proper way to work with UI from the asynchronous code. We will learn what a task scheduler is, why it is so important, how it can harm our application, and how to use it to avoid errors.

Getting ready

To step through this recipe, you will need Visual Studio 2012. There are no other prerequisites. The source code for this recipe can be found at `BookSamples\Chapter4\Recipe9`.

How to do it...

For tweaking tasks execution with `TaskScheduler`, perform the following steps:

1. Start Visual Studio 2012. Create a new C# **WPF Application** project. This time we will need a UI thread with a message loop, which is not available in console applications.

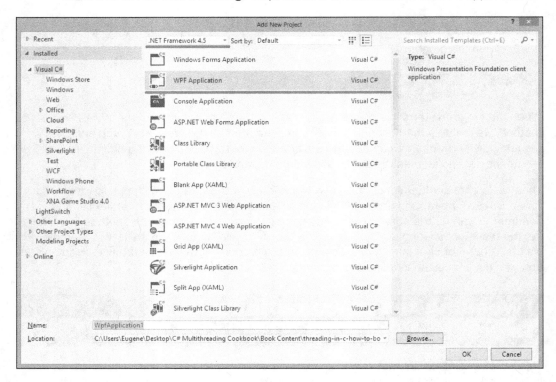

2. In the `MainWindow.xaml` file, add the following markup inside a grid element (that is, between the `<Grid>` and `</Grid>` tags):

```
<TextBlock Name="ContentTextBlock"
HorizontalAlignment="Left"
Margin="44,134,0,0"
VerticalAlignment="Top"
Width="425"
Height="40"/>
<Button Content="Sync"
HorizontalAlignment="Left"
Margin="45,190,0,0"
VerticalAlignment="Top"
Width="75"
```

```
Click="ButtonSync_Click"/>
<Button Content="Async"
HorizontalAlignment="Left"
Margin="165,190,0,0"
VerticalAlignment="Top"
Width="75"
Click="ButtonAsync_Click"/>
<Button Content="Async OK"

HorizontalAlignment="Left"

Margin="285,190,0,0"

VerticalAlignment="Top"

Width="75"

Click="ButtonAsyncOK_Click"/>
```

3. In the `MainWindow.xaml.cs` file, use the following `using` directives:

```
using System;
using System.Threading;
using System.Threading.Tasks;
using System.Windows;
using System.Windows.Input;
```

4. Add the following code snippet below the `MainWindow` constructor:

```
void ButtonSync_Click(object sender, RoutedEventArgs e){
  ContentTextBlock.Text = string.Empty;
  try {
    //string result = TaskMethod(TaskScheduler.
    //FromCurrentSynchronizationContext()).Result;
    string result = TaskMethod().Result;
    ContentTextBlock.Text = result;
  }
  catch (Exception ex) {
    ContentTextBlock.Text = ex.InnerException.Message;
  }
}

void ButtonAsync_Click(object sender, RoutedEventArgs e) {
  ContentTextBlock.Text = string.Empty;
  Mouse.OverrideCursor = Cursors.Wait;
  Task<string> task = TaskMethod();
  task.ContinueWith(t => {
    ContentTextBlock.Text = t.Exception.InnerException.
      Message;
```

```
      Mouse.OverrideCursor = null;
    },
    CancellationToken.None, TaskContinuationOptions.
      OnlyOnFaulted,
    TaskScheduler.FromCurrentSynchronizationContext());
}

void ButtonAsyncOK_Click(object sender, RoutedEventArgs e){
  ContentTextBlock.Text = string.Empty;
  Mouse.OverrideCursor = Cursors.Wait;
  Task<string> task = TaskMethod(TaskScheduler.
    FromCurrentSynchronizationContext());
  task.ContinueWith(t =>Mouse.OverrideCursor = null,
    CancellationToken.None,
    TaskContinuationOptions.None,
    TaskScheduler.FromCurrentSynchronizationContext());
}

Task<string> TaskMethod() {
  return TaskMethod(TaskScheduler.Default);
}

Task<string> TaskMethod(TaskScheduler scheduler) {
  Task delay = Task.Delay(TimeSpan.FromSeconds(5));

  return delay.ContinueWith(t => {
    string str = string.Format("Task is running on a thread
      id {0}. Is thread pool thread: {1}",
        Thread.CurrentThread.ManagedThreadId,
          Thread.CurrentThread.IsThreadPoolThread);
    ContentTextBlock.Text = str;
    return str;
  }, scheduler);
}
```

5. Run the program.

How it works...

Here we meet many new things. First, we created a WPF application instead of a console application. It is necessary because we need a user interface thread with a message loop to demonstrate the different options of running a task asynchronously.

There is a very important abstraction called `TaskScheduler`. This component is actually responsible for how the task will be executed. The default task scheduler puts tasks on a thread pool worker thread. This is the most common scenario and there's no surprise that it is the default option in TPL. We also know how to run a task synchronously and how to attach them to the parent tasks to run those tasks together. Now let us see what else we can do with tasks.

When the program starts, we create a window with three buttons. The first button invokes a synchronous task execution. The code is placed inside the `ButtonSync_Click` method. While the task runs, even we are not able to move the application window. The user interface is totally frozen while the user interface thread is busy running the task, and cannot respond to any message loop until the task is complete. This is quite a common bad practice for GUI Windows application, and we need to find a way to work around this issue.

The second problem is that we try to access the UI controls from another thread. The graphical user interface controls have never been designed to be used from multiple threads, and to avoid possible errors, you are not allowed to access these components from a thread other than the one on which it was created. When we try to do that, we get an exception, and the exception message is printed on the main window in 5 seconds.

To resolve the first problem, we try to run the task asynchronously. This is what the second button does; the code for this is placed inside the `ButtonAsync_Click` method. If you run the task under debugger, you will see that it is placed on a thread pool, and in the end, we will get the same exception. However, the user interface remains responsive all the time while the task runs. This is a good thing, but we need to get rid of the exception.

And we already did that! To output the error message, a continuation was provided with the `TaskScheduler.FromCurrentSynchronizationContext` option. If this is not done, we would not see the error message because we would get the same exception that happened inside the task. This option instructs the TPL infrastructure to put a code inside the continuation on the UI thread and run it asynchronously with a help of the UI thread message loop. This resolves the problem with accessing UI controls from another thread, but still keeps our UI responsive.

To check if it is true, we press the last button that runs the code inside the `ButtonAsyncOK_Click` method. All that is different is that we provide the UI thread task scheduler to our task. After the task completes, you will see that it runs on the UI thread in an asynchronous manner. The UI remains responsive, and it is even possible to press another button despite the wait cursor being active.

However, there are some tricks for using the UI thread for running tasks. If we go back to the synchronous task code and uncomment the line with getting the result with the UI thread task scheduler provided, we will never get any result. This is a classical deadlock situation: we are dispatching an operation in the queue of the UI thread and the UI thread waits for this operation to complete, but as it waits, it cannot run the operation, which will never end (not even start). This will also happen if we call the `Wait` method on task. To avoid the deadlock, never use the synchronous operations on task scheduled to the UI thread; just use `ContinueWith`, or `async/await` from C# 5.0.

5
Using C# 5.0

In this chapter, we will look through the native asynchronous programming support in the C# 5.0 programming language. You will learn about the following:

- ▶ Using the await operator to get asynchronous task results
- ▶ Using the await operator in a lambda expression
- ▶ Using the await operator with consequent asynchronous tasks
- ▶ Using the await operator for the execution of parallel asynchronous tasks
- ▶ Handling exceptions in asynchronous operations
- ▶ Avoid using the captured synchronization context
- ▶ Working around the async void method
- ▶ Designing a custom awaitable type
- ▶ Using the dynamic type with await

Introduction

Until now, we learned about Task Parallel Library, the latest asynchronous programming infrastructure from Microsoft. It allows us to design our program in a modular manner, combining different asynchronous operations together.

Unfortunately, it is still difficult to understand the actual program flow when reading such a program. In a large program, there will be numerous tasks and continuations that depend on each other, continuations that run other continuations, continuations for exception handling, and they are all gathered together in the program code in very different places. Therefore, to understand the sequence of which operation goes first and what happens next becomes a very challenging problem.

Another issue to watch out for is to see if the proper synchronization context is propagated to each asynchronous task that could touch user interface controls. It is only permitted to use these controls from the UI thread; else, we would get a multithreaded access exception.

Speaking about exceptions, we also have to use separate continuation tasks to handle errors that occur inside the antecedent asynchronous operation or operations. This in turn results in complicated error-handling code that is spread through different parts in the code, not logically related to each other.

To address these issues, the authors of C# 5.0 introduced new language enhancements called **asynchronous functions**. They really make asynchronous programming simple, but at the same time, it is a higher-level abstraction over TPL. As we mentioned in *Chapter 4, Using Task Parallel Library*, abstraction hides important implementation details and makes asynchronous programming easier at the cost of taking away many important things from the programmer. It is very important to understand the concept behind asynchronous functions to create robust and scalable applications.

To create an asynchronous function, first you mark a method with the `async` keyword. It is not possible to have the async property or event accessor methods and constructors without first doing this. The code will look as follows:

```
async Task<string> GetStringAsync()
{
    await Task.Delay(TimeSpan.FromSeconds(2));
    return "Hello, World!";
}
```

Another important fact is that asynchronous functions must return the `Task` or `Task<T>` type. It is possible to have the `async void` methods, but it is preferable to use the `async Task` method instead. The only reasonable option to use `async void` functions is when using top-level UI control event handlers in your application.

Inside a method marked with the `async` keyword, you can use the `await` operator. This operator works with tasks from TPL and gets the result of the asynchronous operation inside the task. The details will be covered later in the chapter. You cannot use the `await` operator outside the `async` method; there will be a compilation error. In addition, asynchronous functions should have at least one `await` operator inside its code. However, it will lead to just a compilation warning, not an error.

It is important to note that this method returns immediately after the line with the `await` call. In case of synchronous execution, the executing thread will be blocked for 2 seconds and then return a result. Here, we wait asynchronously while returning a worker thread to a thread pool, immediately after executing the `await` operator. After 2 seconds, we get the worker thread from a thread pool once again and run the rest of the asynchronous method on it. This allows us to re-use this worker thread to do some other work while these 2 seconds pass, which is extremely important for application scalability. With the help of asynchronous functions we have a linear program control flow, but it is still asynchronous. This is both very comfortable and very confusing. The recipes in this chapter will help you to learn every important aspect of asynchronous functions.

From my experience, there is a common misunderstanding about how programs work if there are two consecutive `await` operators in it. Many people think that if we use the `await` function on one asynchronous operation after another, they run in parallel. However, they actually run sequentially; the second one starts only when the first operation completes. It is very important to remember this, and later in the chapter, we will cover this topic in detail.

There are a number of limitations connected with using `async` and `await` in C# 5.0. For example, it is not possible to mark the console application's `Main` method as `async`; you cannot have the `await` operator inside a `catch`, `finally`, `lock`, or `unsafe` block. It is not allowed to have `ref` and `out` parameters on an asynchronous function. There are more subtleties, but these are the major points.

Asynchronous functions are turned into complex program constructs by the C# compiler behind the scenes. I intentionally will not describe this in detail; the resulting code is quite similar to another C# construct, called **iterators**, and is implemented as a sort of state machine. Since many developers have started to use the `async` modifier almost on every method, I would like to emphasize that there is no sense in marking a method as `async` if it is not intended to be used in an asynchronous or parallel manner. Calling the `async` method includes a significant performance hit, and the usual method call is going to be about 40 to 50 times faster as compared to the same method marked with the `async` keyword. Please be aware of that.

In this chapter, we will learn to use the C# 5.0 `async` and `await` keywords to work with asynchronous operations. We will cover how to await the asynchronous operations sequentially and in parallel. We will discuss how to use `await` in lambda expressions, how to handle exceptions, and how to avoid pitfalls when using the `async void` methods. To conclude the chapter, we will dive deep into synchronization context propagation and learn how to create our own awaitable objects instead of using tasks.

Using the await operator to get asynchronous task results

This recipe walks through the basic scenario of using asynchronous functions. We will compare how to get an asynchronous operation result with TPL and with the `await` operator.

Getting ready

To step through this recipe, you will need Visual Studio 2012. There are no other prerequisites. The source code for this recipe can be found at `BookSamples\Chapter5\Recipe1`.

How to do it...

To use the `await` operator to get asynchronous task results, perform the following steps:

1. Start Visual Studio 2012. Create a new C# **Console Application** project.

2. In the `Program.cs` file, add the following `using` directives:

    ```
    using System;
    using System.Threading;
    using System.Threading.Tasks;
    ```

3. Add the following code snippet below the `Main` method:

    ```
    static Task AsynchronyWithTPL()
    {
      Task<string> t = GetInfoAsync("Task 1");
      Task t2 = t.ContinueWith(task => Console.WriteLine(
        t.Result), TaskContinuationOptions.NotOnFaulted);
      Task t3 = t.ContinueWith(task => Console.WriteLine(
        t.Exception.InnerException), TaskContinuationOptions.
          OnlyOnFaulted);

      return Task.WhenAny(t2, t3);
    }

    async static Task AsynchronyWithAwait()
    {
      try
      {
        string result = await GetInfoAsync("Task 2");
        Console.WriteLine(result);
      }
    ```

```
    catch (Exception ex)
    {
      Console.WriteLine(ex);
    }
  }

  async static Task<string> GetInfoAsync(string name)
  {
    await Task.Delay(TimeSpan.FromSeconds(2));
    //throw new Exception("Boom!");

    return string.Format("Task {0} is running on a thread id
      {1}. Is thread pool thread: {2}", name,
        Thread.CurrentThread.ManagedThreadId,
          Thread.CurrentThread.IsThreadPoolThread);
  }
```

4. Add the following code snippet inside the `Main` method:

```
Task t = AsynchronyWithTPL();
t.Wait();

t = AsynchronyWithAwait();
t.Wait();
```

5. Run the program.

How it works...

When the program runs, we run two asynchronous operations. One of them is standard TPL-powered code, and the second one uses the new `async` and `await` C# features. The `AsynchronyWithTPL` method starts a task that runs for 2 seconds and then returns a string with information about the worker thread. Then, we define a continuation to print out the asynchronous operation result after the operation completes, and another one to print the exception details in case errors occur. Finally, we return a task representing one of the continuation tasks, and wait for its completion in the `Main` method.

In the `AsynchronyWithAwait` method, we achieve the same result by using `await` with the task. It is as if we write just usual synchronous code – we get the result from the task, print out the result, and catch an exception if the task is completed with errors. The key difference is that we actually have an asynchronous program. Immediately after using `await`, C# creates a task that has a continuation task with all the remaining code after the `await` operator, and deals with exception propagation as well. Then, we return this task to the `Main` method and wait until it completes.

 Please note that depending on the nature of the underlying asynchronous operation and the current synchronization context, the exact means of executing the asynchronous code may differ. We will explain this later in the chapter.

Therefore, we can see that the first and the second parts of the program are conceptually equivalent, but in the second part the C# compiler does the work of handling asynchronous code implicitly. It is, in fact, even more complicated than the first part, and we will cover the details in the next few recipes of this chapter.

Please remember that it is not recommended to use the `Task.Wait` and `Task.Result` methods in environments, such as Windows GUI or ASP.NET. This could lead to deadlocks if the programmer is not 100% aware of what is really going on in the code. This was illustrated in the *Tweaking tasks execution with TaskScheduler* recipe of *Chapter 4, Using Task Parallel Library*, when we used `Task.Result` in the WPF application.

To test how exception handling works, just uncomment the `throw new Exception` line inside the `GetInfoAsync` method.

Using the await operator in a lambda expression

This recipe will show how to use `await` inside a lambda expression. We will write an anonymous method that uses `await`, and get a result of the method execution asynchronously.

Getting ready

To step through this recipe, you will need Visual Studio 2012. There are no other prerequisites. The source code for this recipe can be found at `BookSamples\Chapter5\Recipe2`.

How to do it...

To write an anonymous method that uses `await` and get a result of the method execution asynchronously by using the `await` operator in a lambda expression, perform the following steps:

1. Start Visual Studio 2012. Create a new C# **Console Application** project.

2. In the `Program.cs` file, add the following `using` directives:

```
using System;
using System.Threading;
using System.Threading.Tasks;
```

3. Add the following code snippet below the `Main` method:

```
async static Task AsynchronousProcessing()
{
  Func<string, Task<string>> asyncLambda = async name => {
    await Task.Delay(TimeSpan.FromSeconds(2));
    return string.Format("Task {0} is running on a thread
      id {1}. Is thread pool thread: {2}", name,
        Thread.CurrentThread.ManagedThreadId,
          Thread.CurrentThread.IsThreadPoolThread);
  };

  string result = await asyncLambda("async lambda");

  Console.WriteLine(result);
}
```

4. Add the following code snippet inside the `Main` method:

```
Task t = AsynchronousProcessing();
t.Wait();
```

5. Run the program.

How it works...

First, we move out the asynchronous function into the `AsynchronousProcessing` method since we cannot use `async` with `Main`. Then, we describe a lambda expression using the `async` keyword. As the type of any lambda expression cannot be inferred from the lambda itself, we have to specify its type to the C# compiler explicitly. In our case, the type means that our lambda accepts one string parameter, and returns a `Task<string>` object.

Then, we define the lambda expression body. One aberration is that the method is defined to return a `Task<string>` object, but we actually return a string, and get no compilation errors! The C# compiler automatically generates a task and returns it for us.

The last step is to await the asynchronous lambda expression execution and print out the result.

Using the await operator with consequent asynchronous tasks

This recipe will show how exactly the program flows when we have several consecutive `await` methods in the code. We will learn how to read the code with the `await` methods and understand why the `await` call is an asynchronous operation.

Getting ready

To step through this recipe, you will need Visual Studio 2012. There are no other prerequisites. The source code for this recipe can be found at `BookSamples\Chapter5\Recipe3`.

How to do it...

To understand a program flow in the presence of consecutive `await` methods, perform the following steps:

1. Start Visual Studio 2012. Create a new C# **Console Application** project.

2. In the `Program.cs` file, add the following `using` directives:

```
using System;
using System.Threading;
using System.Threading.Tasks;
```

3. Add the following code snippet below the `Main` method:

```
static Task AsynchronyWithTPL()
{
  var containerTask = new Task(() => {
    Task<string> t = GetInfoAsync("TPL 1");
    t.ContinueWith(task => {
      Console.WriteLine(t.Result);
      Task<string> t2 = GetInfoAsync("TPL 2");
      t2.ContinueWith(innerTask =>
        Console.WriteLine(innerTask.Result),
          TaskContinuationOptions.NotOnFaulted |
            TaskContinuationOptions.AttachedToParent);
      t2.ContinueWith(innerTask =>
        Console.WriteLine(innerTask.Exception.
          InnerException),
            TaskContinuationOptions.OnlyOnFaulted |
              TaskContinuationOptions.AttachedToParent);
      },
      TaskContinuationOptions.NotOnFaulted |
        TaskContinuationOptions.AttachedToParent);

    t.ContinueWith(task =>
      Console.WriteLine(t.Exception.InnerException),
        TaskContinuationOptions.OnlyOnFaulted |
          TaskContinuationOptions.AttachedToParent);
  });

  containerTask.Start();
  return containerTask;
}

async static Task AsynchronyWithAwait()
{
  try
  {
    string result = await GetInfoAsync("Async 1");
    Console.WriteLine(result);
    result = await GetInfoAsync("Async 2");
    Console.WriteLine(result);
  }
  catch (Exception ex)
  {
    Console.WriteLine(ex);
  }
}
```

```
async static Task<string> GetInfoAsync(string name)
{
    Console.WriteLine("Task {0} started!", name);
    await Task.Delay(TimeSpan.FromSeconds(2));
    if(name == "TPL 2")
        throw new Exception("Boom!");
    return string.Format("Task {0} is running on a thread id
        {1}. Is thread pool thread: {2}",
            name, Thread.CurrentThread.ManagedThreadId,
                Thread.CurrentThread.IsThreadPoolThread);
}
```

4. Add the following code snippet inside the `Main` method:

```
Task t = AsynchronyWithTPL();
t.Wait();

t = AsynchronyWithAwait();
t.Wait();
```

5. Run the program.

How it works...

When the program runs, we run two asynchronous operations just as in the first recipe. However, this time we shall start from the `AsynchronyWithAwait` method. It still looks like the usual synchronous code; the only difference is the two `await` statements. The most important point is that the code is still sequential, and the `Async 2` task will start only after the previous one completes. When we read the code, the program flow is very clear: we see what runs first, and what goes after. Then, how is this program asynchronous? Well, first, it is not always asynchronous. If a task is already complete when we use `await`, we will get its result synchronously. Otherwise, the common approach when we see an `await` statement inside the code is to note that at this point the method will return immediately and the rest of the code will be run in a continuation task. Since we do not block the execution waiting for the result of an operation, it is an asynchronous call. Instead of calling `t.Wait` in the `Main` method, we can perform any other task, while the code in `AsynchronyWithAwait` method is executing. However, the main thread must wait until all the asynchronous operations complete, or they will be stopped as they run on background threads.

The `AsynchronyWithTPL` method imitates the same program flow as the `AsynchronyWithAwait` method does. We need a container task to handle all the dependent tasks together. Then, we start the main task, and add a set of continuations to it. When the task is complete, we print out the result; we then start one more task, which in turn has more continuations to continue work after the second task completes. To test the exception handling, we throw an exception on purpose when running the second task and get its information printed out. This set of continuations creates the same program flow as in the first method, and when we compare it to the code with the `await` methods, we can see that it is much easier to read and understand. The only trick is to remember that asynchrony does not always mean parallel execution.

Using the await operator for the execution of parallel asynchronous tasks execution

In this recipe, we will learn how to use `await` to run asynchronous operations in parallel instead of the usual sequential execution.

Getting ready

To step through this recipe, you will need Visual Studio 2012. There are no other prerequisites. The source code for this recipe can be found at `BookSamples\Chapter5\Recipe4`.

How to do it...

To understand the use of `await` operator for parallel asynchronous tasks execution, perform the following steps:

1. Start Visual Studio 2012. Create a new C# **Console Application** project.

2. In the `Program.cs` file, add the following `using` directives:

```
using System;
using System.Threading;
using System.Threading.Tasks;
```

3. Add the following code below the `Main` method:

```
async static Task AsynchronousProcessing()
{
  Task<string> t1 = GetInfoAsync("Task 1", 3);
  Task<string> t2 = GetInfoAsync("Task 2", 5);

  string[] results = await Task.WhenAll(t1, t2);
  foreach (string result in results)
  {
    Console.WriteLine(result);
  }
}

async static Task<string> GetInfoAsync(string name, int seconds)
{
  await Task.Delay(TimeSpan.FromSeconds(seconds));
  /*await Task.Run(() =>
    Thread.Sleep(TimeSpan.FromSeconds(seconds)));*/
  return string.Format("Task {0} is running on a thread id
    {1}. Is thread pool thread: {2}", name,
      Thread.CurrentThread.ManagedThreadId,
        Thread.CurrentThread.IsThreadPoolThread);
}
```

4. Add the following code snippet inside the `Main` method:

```
Task t = AsynchronousProcessing();
t.Wait();
```

5. Run the program.

How it works...

Here we define two asynchronous tasks running for 3 and 5 seconds respectively. Then, we use a `Task.WhenAll` helper method to create another task that will complete only when all of the underlying tasks complete. Then, we await the result of this combined task. After 5 seconds, we get all the results, which means that the tasks were running simultaneously.

However, there is one interesting observation. When you run the program, you might notice that both tasks are likely to be served by the same worker thread from a thread pool. How is that possible when we have run the tasks in parallel? To make things even more interesting, let's comment out the `await Task.Delay` line inside the `GetIntroAsync` method and uncomment the `await Task.Run` line, and then run the program.

We will see that in this case both the tasks will be served by different worker threads. The difference is that `Task.Delay` uses a timer under the hood, and the processing goes as follows: we get the worker thread from a thread pool, which awaits the `Task.Delay` method to return a result. Then, the `Task.Delay` method starts the timer and specifies a piece of code that will be called when the timer counts the number of seconds specified to the `Task.Delay` method. Then we immediately return the worker thread to a thread pool. When the timer event runs, we get any available worker thread from a thread pool once again (which could be the same thread we used first) and run the code provided to the timer on it.

When we use the `Task.Run` method, we get a worker thread from a thread pool and make it block for a number of seconds, provided to the `Thread.Sleep` method. Then, we get a second worker thread and block it as well. In this scenario, we consume two worker threads and they do absolutely nothing, not being able to perform any other task while waiting.

We will talk in detail about the first scenario in *Chapter 9*, *Using asynchronous I/O*, where we will discuss a large set of asynchronous operations working with data inputs and outputs. Using the first approach whenever possible is the key to creating scalable server applications.

Handling exceptions in the asynchronous operations

This recipe will describe how to deal with exception handling using asynchronous functions in C#. We will learn how to work with aggregate exceptions in case you use `await` with multiple parallel asynchronous operations.

Getting ready

To step through this recipe, you will need Visual Studio 2012. There are no other prerequisites. The source code for this recipe can be found at `BookSamples\Chapter5\Recipe5`.

How to do it...

To understand handling exceptions in asynchronous operations, perform the following steps:

1. Start Visual Studio 2012. Create a new C# **Console Application** project.

2. In the `Program.cs` file, add the following `using` directives:

   ```
   using System;
   using System.Threading;
   using System.Threading.Tasks;
   ```

3. Add the following code snippet below the `Main` method:

```csharp
async static Task AsynchronousProcessing()
{
  Console.WriteLine("1. Single exception");

  try
  {
    string result = await GetInfoAsync("Task 1", 2);
    Console.WriteLine(result);
  }
  catch (Exception ex)
  {
    Console.WriteLine("Exception details: {0}", ex);
  }

  Console.WriteLine();
  Console.WriteLine("2. Multiple exceptions");

  Task<string> t1 = GetInfoAsync("Task 1", 3);
  Task<string> t2 = GetInfoAsync("Task 2", 2);
  try
  {
    string[] results = await Task.WhenAll(t1, t2);
    Console.WriteLine(results.Length);
  }
  catch (Exception ex)
  {
    Console.WriteLine("Exception details: {0}", ex);
  }

  Console.WriteLine();
  Console.WriteLine("2. Multiple exceptions with
AggregateException");

  t1 = GetInfoAsync("Task 1", 3);
  t2 = GetInfoAsync("Task 2", 2);
  Task<string[]> t3 = Task.WhenAll(t1, t2);
  try
  {
    string[] results = await t3;
    Console.WriteLine(results.Length);
  }
  catch
  {
    var ae = t3.Exception.Flatten();
    var exceptions = ae.InnerExceptions;
    Console.WriteLine("Exceptions caught: {0}", exceptions.Count);
    foreach (var e in exceptions)
    {
```

```
      Console.WriteLine("Exception details: {0}", e);
      Console.WriteLine();
    }
  }
}

async static Task<string> GetInfoAsync(string name, int seconds)
{
  await Task.Delay(TimeSpan.FromSeconds(seconds));
  throw new Exception(string.Format("Boom from {0}!", name));
}
```

4. Add the following code snippet inside the `Main` method:

```
Task t = AsynchronousProcessing();
t.Wait();
```

5. Run the program.

How it works...

We run three scenarios to illustrate the most common cases of error handling using `async` and `await` in C#. The first case is very simple, and almost identical to the usual synchronous code. We just use the `try/catch` statement and get the exception's details.

A very common mistake is using the same approach when more than one asynchronous operation is being awaited. If we use the `catch` block the same way as before, we will get only the first exception from the underlying `AggregateException` object.

To collect all the information, we have to use the awaited tasks' `Exception` property. In the third scenario, we flatten the `AggregateException` hierarchy, and then unwrap all the underlying exceptions from it using the `Flatten` method of `AggregateException`.

Avoid using the captured synchronization context

This recipe talks about the details of synchronization context behavior when `await` is used to get asynchronous operation results. We will learn how and when to turn off the synchronization context flow.

Getting ready

To step through this recipe, you will need Visual Studio 2012. There are no other prerequisites. The source code for this recipe can be found at `BookSamples\Chapter5\Recipe6`.

How to do it...

To understand details of synchronization context behavior when `await` is used and to learn how and when to turn off the synchronization context flow, perform the following steps:

1. Start Visual Studio 2012. Create a new C# **Console Application** project.

2. Add references to Windows Presentation Foundation Library.

    1. Right-click on the **References** folder in the project, and select the **Add reference...** menu option.

    2. Add references to the following libraries: **PresentationCore**, **PresentationFramework**, **System.Xaml**, and **Windows.Base**. You can use the search function in the reference manager dialog as follows:

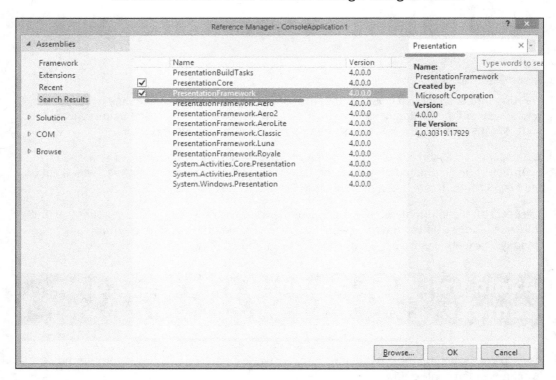

3. In the `Program.cs` file, add the following `using` directives:

```
using System;
using System.Diagnostics;
using System.Text;
using System.Threading.Tasks;
using System.Windows;
using System.Windows.Controls;
```

4. Add the following code snippet below the `Main` method:

```
private static Label _label;

async static void Click(object sender, EventArgs e)
{
  _label.Content = new TextBlock {Text = "Calculating..."};
  TimeSpan resultWithContext = await Test();
  TimeSpan resultNoContext = await TestNoContext();
  /*TimeSpan resultNoContext = await
    TestNoContext().ConfigureAwait(false);*/
  var sb = new StringBuilder();
  sb.AppendLine(string.Format("With the context: {0}",
    resultWithContext));
  sb.AppendLine(string.Format("Without the context: {0}",
    resultNoContext));
  sb.AppendLine(string.Format("Ratio: {0:0.00}",
    resultWithContext.TotalMilliseconds/resultNoContext.
      TotalMilliseconds));
  _label.Content = new TextBlock {Text = sb.ToString()};
}

async static Task<TimeSpan> Test()
{
  const int iterationsNumber = 100000;
  var sw = new Stopwatch();
  sw.Start();
  for (int i = 0; i < iterationsNumber; i++)
  {
    var t = Task.Run(() => { });
    await t;
  }
  sw.Stop();
  return sw.Elapsed;
}

async static Task<TimeSpan> TestNoContext()
{
  const int iterationsNumber = 100000;
  var sw = new Stopwatch();
  sw.Start();
  for (int i = 0; i < iterationsNumber; i++)
  {
    var t = Task.Run(() => { });
    await t.ConfigureAwait(
      continueOnCapturedContext: false);
  }
  sw.Stop();
  return sw.Elapsed;
}
```

5. Replace the `Main` method with the following code snippet:

```
[STAThread]
static void Main(string[] args)
{
    var app = new Application();
    var win = new Window();
    var panel = new StackPanel();
    var button = new Button();
    _label = new Label();
    _label.FontSize = 32;
    _label.Height = 200;
    button.Height = 100;
    button.FontSize = 32;
    button.Content = new TextBlock {
        Text = "Start asynchronous operations"};
    button.Click += Click;
    panel.Children.Add(_label);
    panel.Children.Add(button);
    win.Content = panel;
    app.Run(win);

    Console.ReadLine();
}
```

6. Run the program.

How it works...

In this example, we will study one of the most important aspects of an asynchronous function's default behavior. We already know about task schedulers and synchronization contexts from *Chapter 4, Using Task Parallel Library*. By default, the `await` operator tries to capture synchronization contexts, and executes the following code on it. As we already know, this helps us write asynchronous code by working with user interface controls. In addition, deadlock situations like those that were described in the previous chapter will not happen when using `await`, since we do not block the UI thread while waiting for the result.

It is reasonable, but let's see what can potentially happen. In this example, we create a Windows Presentation Foundation application programmatically and subscribe to its button-click event. When clicking the button, we run two asynchronous operations. One of them uses a regular `await` operator while the other uses the `ConfigureAwait` method with `false` as a parameter value. It explicitly instructs that we should not use captured synchronization contexts to run continuation code on it. Inside each operation, we measure the time they take to complete, and then we display the respective time and ratios on the main screen.

As a result, we see that the regular `await` operator takes much more time to complete. This is because we post one hundred thousand continuation tasks on the UI thread, which uses its message loop to asynchronously work with those tasks. In this case, we do not need this code to run on the UI thread, since we do not access the UI components from the asynchronous operation; using `ConfigureAwait` with `false` will be a much more efficient solution.

There is one more thing worth noting. Try to run the program by just clicking on the button and waiting for the results. Now do the same thing again, but this time click on the button and try to drag the application window from side-to-side in a random manner. You will notice that the code on the captured synchronization context becomes slower! This funny side-effect perfectly illustrates how dangerous asynchronous programming is. It is very easy to experience a situation like this, and it would be almost impossible to debug if you have never experienced such a behavior before.

To be fair, let's see the opposite scenario. In the preceding code snippet, inside the `Click` method, uncomment the commented line and comment its immediately preceding line. When running the application, we will get a multithreaded control access exception, because the code that sets the `Label` control text will not be posted on the captured context, but will be executed on a thread pool worker thread instead.

Working around the async void method

This recipe describes why `async void` methods are quite dangerous to use. We will learn in what situations it is acceptable to use this method, and what to use instead when possible.

Getting ready

To step through this recipe, you will need Visual Studio 2012. There are no other prerequisites. The source code for this recipe can be found at `BookSamples\Chapter5\Recipe7`.

How to do it...

To learn how to work with the `async void` method, perform the following steps:

1. Start Visual Studio 2012. Create a new C# **Console Application** project.

2. In the `Program.cs` file, add the following `using` directives:

```
using System;
using System.Threading;
using System.Threading.Tasks;
```

3. Add the following code snippet below the `Main` method:

```csharp
async static Task AsyncTaskWithErrors()
{
  string result = await GetInfoAsync("AsyncTaskException",
    2);
  Console.WriteLine(result);
}

async static void AsyncVoidWithErrors()
{
  string result = await GetInfoAsync("AsyncVoidException",
    2);
  Console.WriteLine(result);
}

async static Task AsyncTask()
{
  string result = await GetInfoAsync("AsyncTask", 2);
  Console.WriteLine(result);
}

private static async void AsyncVoid()
{
  string result = await GetInfoAsync("AsyncVoid", 2);
  Console.WriteLine(result);
}

async static Task<string> GetInfoAsync(string name,
  int seconds)
{
  await Task.Delay(TimeSpan.FromSeconds(seconds));
  if(name.Contains("Exception"))
    throw new Exception(string.Format("Boom from {0}!",
      name));
  return string.Format("Task {0} is running on a thread id
    {1}. Is thread pool thread: {2}", name,
      Thread.CurrentThread.ManagedThreadId,
        Thread.CurrentThread.IsThreadPoolThread);
}
```

4. Add the following code snippet inside the `Main` method:

```
Task t = AsyncTask();
t.Wait();

AsyncVoid();
Thread.Sleep(TimeSpan.FromSeconds(3));

t = AsyncTaskWithErrors();
while(!t.IsFaulted)
{
  Thread.Sleep(TimeSpan.FromSeconds(1));
}
Console.WriteLine(t.Exception);

//try
//{
//  AsyncVoidWithErrors();
//  Thread.Sleep(TimeSpan.FromSeconds(3));
//}
//catch (Exception ex)
//{
//  Console.WriteLine(ex);
//}

//int[] numbers = new[] {1, 2, 3, 4, 5};
//Array.ForEach(numbers, async number => {
//  await Task.Delay(TimeSpan.FromSeconds(1));
//  if (number == 3) throw new Exception("Boom!");
//  Console.WriteLine(number);
//});

Console.ReadLine();
```

5. Run the program.

How it works...

When the program starts, we start two asynchronous operations by calling the two methods, `AsyncTask` and `AsyncVoid`. The first method returns a `Task` object while the other returns nothing since it is declared as `async void`. They both return immediately since they are asynchronous, but then the first one can be easily monitored with the returned task status or just by calling the `Wait` method on it. The only way to wait for the second method to complete is to literally wait for some time because we have not declared any object we can use to monitor the state of the asynchronous operation. Of course, it is possible to use some kind of shared state variable and set it from the `async void` method while checking it from the `calling` method, but it is better to just return a `Task` object instead.

The most dangerous part is exception handling. In case of the `async void` method, the exception handling methods will be posted to a current synchronization context; in our case, a thread pool. An unhandled exception on a thread pool will terminate the whole process. It is possible to intercept unhandled exceptions using the `AppDomain.UnhandledException` event, but there is no way to recover the process from there. To experience this, we should uncomment the `try/catch` block inside the `Main` method, and then run the program.

Another fact about using the `async void` lambda expressions: they are compatible with the `Action` type, which is being widely used in the standard .NET Framework class library. It is very easy to forget about exception handling inside this lambda, which will crash the program again. To see an example of this, uncomment the second commented-out block inside the `Main` method.

I strongly recommended using `async void` only in UI event handlers. In all other situations, use the methods that return `Task` instead.

Designing a custom awaitable type

This recipe shows how to design a very basic awaitable type that is compatible with the `await` operator.

Getting ready

To step through this recipe, you will need Visual Studio 2012. There are no other prerequisites. The source code for this recipe can be found at `BookSamples\Chapter5\Recipe8`.

How to do it...

For designing a custom awaitable type, perform the following steps:

1. Start Visual Studio 2012. Create a new C# **Console Application** project.

2. In the `Program.cs` file, add the following `using` directives:
```
using System;
using System.Runtime.CompilerServices;
using System.Threading;
using System.Threading.Tasks;
```

3. Add the following code snippet below the `Main` method:
```
async static Task AsynchronousProcessing()
{
  var sync = new CustomAwaitable(true);
  string result = await sync;
  Console.WriteLine(result);

  var async = new CustomAwaitable(false);
  result = await async;

  Console.WriteLine(result);
}

class CustomAwaitable
{
  public CustomAwaitable(bool completeSynchronously)
  {
    _completeSynchronously = completeSynchronously;
  }

  public CustomAwaiter GetAwaiter()
  {
    return new CustomAwaiter(_completeSynchronously);
  }

  private readonly bool _completeSynchronously;
}

class CustomAwaiter : INotifyCompletion
{
  private string _result = "Completed synchronously";
  private readonly bool _completeSynchronously;

  public bool IsCompleted { get {
    return _completeSynchronously; } }
```

```
      public CustomAwaiter(bool completeSynchronously)
      {
        _completeSynchronously = completeSynchronously;
      }

      public string GetResult()
      {
        return _result;
      }

      public void OnCompleted(Action continuation)
      {
        ThreadPool.QueueUserWorkItem( state => {
          Thread.Sleep(TimeSpan.FromSeconds(1));
          _result = GetInfo();
          if(continuation != null) continuation();
        });
      }

      private string GetInfo()
      {
        return string.Format("Task is running on a thread id
          {0}. Is thread pool thread: {1}", name,
            Thread.CurrentThread.ManagedThreadId,
              Thread.CurrentThread.IsThreadPoolThread);
      }
    }
```

4. Add the following code snippet inside the `Main` method:

```
Task t = AsynchronousProcessing();
t.Wait();
```

5. Run the program.

How it works...

To be compatible with the `await` operator, a type should comply with a number of requirements, stated in the C# 5.0 specification. If you have Visual Studio 2012 installed, you may find the specifications document inside the `C:\Program Files\Microsoft Visual Studio 11.0\VC#\Specifications\1033` folder (assuming you have used the default installation path).

In paragraph 7.7.7.1, we find a definition of awaitable expressions:

> *The task of an await expression is required to be awaitable. An expression t is awaitable if one of the following holds:*
>
> • *t is of compile time type dynamic*
>
> • *t has an accessible instance or extension method called GetAwaiter with no parameters and no type parameters, and a return type A for which all of the following hold:*
>
> o *A implements the interface System.Runtime.CompilerServices.INotifyCompletion (hereafter known as INotifyCompletion for brevity)*
>
> o *A has an accessible, readable instance property IsCompleted of type bool*
>
> o *A has an accessible instance method GetResult with no parameters and no type parameters*

This information is enough to get started. First, we define an awaitable type `CustomAwaitable` and implement the `GetAwaiter` method, that in turn returns an instance of the `CustomAwaiter` type. `CustomAwaiter` implements the `INotifyCompletion` interface; has the `IsCompleted` property of type `bool`, and has the `GetResult` method, which returns a `string` type. Finally, we write a piece of code that creates two `CustomAwaitable` objects and awaits both of them.

Now we should understand the way `await` expressions are evaluated. This time, the specifications have not been quoted to avoid unnecessary details. Basically, if the `IsCompleted` property returns `true`, we just call the `GetResult` method synchronously. This prevents us from allocating resources for asynchronous task execution if the operation has already been completed. We cover this scenario by providing the `completeSynchronously` parameter to the constructor method of the `CustomAwaitable` object.

Otherwise, we register a callback action to the `OnCompleted` method of `CustomAwaiter` and start the asynchronous operation. When it completes, it calls the provided callback, which will get the result by calling the `GetResult` method on the `CustomAwaiter` object.

 This implementation has been used for educational purposes only. Whenever you write asynchronous functions, the most natural approach is to use the standard `Task` type. You should define your own awaitable type only if you have a solid reason why you cannot use `Task`, and you know exactly what you are doing.

There are many other topics related to designing custom awaitable types, such as the `ICriticalNotifyCompletion` interface implementation and synchronization context propagation. After understanding the basics of how an awaitable type is designed, you will be able to use the C# language specification and other information sources to find out the details you need with ease. But I would like to emphasize that you just use the `Task` type, unless you have a really good reason not to.

Using the dynamic type with await

This recipe shows how to design a very basic type that is compatible with the `await` operator and dynamic C# type.

Getting ready

To step through this recipe, you will need Visual Studio 2012. You will need Internet access to download the NuGet package. There are no other prerequisites. The source code for this recipe can be found at `BookSamples\Chapter5\Recipe9`.

How to do it...

To learn how to use the `dynamic` type with `await`, perform the following steps:

1. Start Visual Studio 2012. Create a new C# **Console Application** project.

2. Add references to the **ImpromptuInterface** NuGet package by following these steps:

    1. Right-click on the **References** folder in the project and select the Manage NuGet Packages... menu option.

    2. Now add your preferred references to the **ImpromptuInterface NuGet** package. You can use the search function in the **Manage NuGet Packages** dialog as follows:

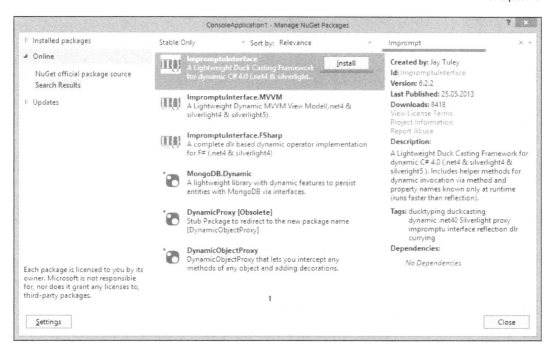

3. In the `Program.cs` file, use the following `using` directives:

```
using System;
using System.Dynamic;
using System.Runtime.CompilerServices;
using System.Threading;
using System.Threading.Tasks;
using ImpromptuInterface;
```

4. Add the following code snippet below the `Main` method:

```csharp
async static Task AsynchronousProcessing()
{
  string result = await GetDynamicAwaitableObject(true);
  Console.WriteLine(result);

  result = await GetDynamicAwaitableObject(false);
  Console.WriteLine(result);
}

static dynamic GetDynamicAwaitableObject(bool
completeSynchronously)
{
  dynamic result = new ExpandoObject();
  dynamic awaiter = new ExpandoObject();

  awaiter.Message = "Completed synchronously";
  awaiter.IsCompleted = completeSynchronously;
  awaiter.GetResult = (Func<string>)(() => awaiter.Message);

  awaiter.OnCompleted = (Action<Action>) ( callback =>
    ThreadPool.QueueUserWorkItem(state => {
      Thread.Sleep(TimeSpan.FromSeconds(1));
      awaiter.Message = GetInfo();
      if (callback != null) callback();
    })
  );

  IAwaiter<string> proxy = Impromptu.ActLike(awaiter);

  result.GetAwaiter = (Func<dynamic>) ( () => proxy );

  return result;
}

static string GetInfo()
{
  return string.Format("Task is running on a thread id {0}.
    Is thread pool thread: {1}",
      Thread.CurrentThread.ManagedThreadId, Thread.CurrentThread.
IsThreadPoolThread);
}

public interface IAwaiter<T> : INotifyCompletion
{
bool IsCompleted { get; }

T GetResult();
}
```

5. Add the following code snippet inside the `Main` method:

```
Task t = AsynchronousProcessing();
t.Wait();
```

6. Run the program.

How it works...

Here, we repeat the trick from the previous recipe, but this time with the help of dynamic expressions. We can achieve this goal with the help of NuGet—a package manager that contains many useful libraries. This time we will use a library that dynamically creates wrappers, implementing the interfaces we need.

To start with, we create two instances of the `ExpandoObject` type and assign them to dynamic local variables. These variables will be our awaitable and awaiter objects. Since an awaitable object just requires having the `GetAwaiter` method, there are no problems with providing it. `ExpandoObject` combined with the `dynamic` keyword allows us to customize it and add properties and methods by assigning corresponding values. It is in fact a dictionary-type collection with keys of type `string` and values of type `object`. If you are familiar with the JavaScript programming language, you might notice that this is very similar to JavaScript objects.

Since `dynamic` allows us to skip compile-time checks in C#, `ExpandoObject` is written in such a way that if you assign something to a property, it creates a dictionary entry, where the key is the property name and a value is any value supplied. When you try to get the property value, it goes into the dictionary and provides the value that is stored in the corresponding dictionary entry. If the value is of the type `Action` or `Func`, we actually store a delegate, which in turn can be used like a method. Therefore, a combination of the `dynamic` type with `ExpandoObject` allows us to create an object and dynamically provide it with properties and methods.

Now, we need to construct our awaiter and awaitable objects. Let's start with the awaiter. First, we provide a property called `Message` and an initial value to this property. Then, we define the `GetResult` method, by using a `Func<string>` type, we assign a lambda expression, which returns the `Message` property value. We next implement the `IsCompleted` property. If it is set to `true`, we can skip the rest of the work and proceed to our awaitable object, stored in the `result` local variable. We just need to add a method returning the `dynamic` object and return our awaiter from it. Then, we can use `result` as the await expression; however, it will run synchronously.

The main challenge is implementing asynchronous processing on our dynamic object. C# language specifications state that an awaiter must implement the `INotifyCompletion` or `ICriticalNotifyCompletion` interface, which `ExpandoObject` does not do. And even when we implement the `OnCompleted` method dynamically, adding it to the awaiter object, we will not succeed because our object does not implement either of the mentioned interfaces.

To work around this problem, we use the `ImpromptuInterface` library that we obtained from NuGet. It allows us to use the `Impromptu.ActLike` method for dynamically creating proxy objects that will implement the required interface. If we try to create a proxy implementing the `INotifyCompletion` interface, we will still fail, because the proxy object is not dynamic anymore, and this interface has the `OnCompleted` method only, but does not have the `IsCompleted` property or the `GetResult` method. As the last workaround, we define a generic interface, `IAwaiter<T>`, which implements `INotifyCompletion` and adds all the required properties and methods. Now, we use it for proxy generation and change the `result` object to return a proxy instead of awaiter from the `GetAwaiter` method. The program now works; we have just constructed an awaitable object that is completely dynamic at runtime.

6
Using Concurrent Collections

In this chapter, we will look through the different data structures for concurrent programming included in the .NET Framework base class library. You will learn about:

- ▶ Using a concurrent dictionary
- ▶ Implementing asynchronous processing using the concurrent queue
- ▶ Changing asynchronous processing order with the concurrent stack
- ▶ Creating a scalable crawler with the concurrent bag
- ▶ Generalizing asynchronous processing with the blocking collection

Introduction

Programming requires understanding and knowledge of basic data structures and algorithms. To choose the best-suited data structure for a concurrent situation, a programmer has to know about many things, such as algorithm time, space complexity, and big O notation. In different well-known scenarios, we always know which data structures are more efficient.

For concurrent computations, we need to have appropriate data structures. These data structures have to be scalable, avoid locks when possible, and at the same time provide thread-safe access. The .NET framework, since Version 4, has the `System.Collections.Concurrent` namespace with several data structures in it. In this chapter, we will cover several data structures and show very simple examples of how to use them.

Let us start with `ConcurrentQueue`. This collection uses atomic **Compare and Swap** (**CAS**) operations and `SpinWait` to ensure thread safety. It implements a **First In First Out** (**FIFO**) collection, which means that the items go out of the queue in the same order in which they were added to the queue. To add an item to a queue you call the `Enqueue` method. The `TryDequeue` method tries to take the first item from the queue, and the `TryPeek` method tries to get the first item without removing it from the queue.

`ConcurrentStack` is also implemented without using any locks with only CAS operations. It is a **Last In First Out** (**LIFO**) collection, which means that the most recently added item will be returned first. To add items you use the `Push` and `PushRange` methods, to retrieve you use `TryPop` and `TryPopRange`, and to inspect you use the `TryPeek` method.

`ConcurrentBag` is an unordered collection that supports duplicate items. It is optimized for a scenario where multiple threads partition their work in such a way that each thread produces and consumes its own tasks, dealing with other threads' tasks very rarely (in which case it uses locks). You add items to a bag with the `Add` method, inspect with `TryPeek`, and take with the `TryTake` method.

Please avoid using the `Count` property on the collections mentioned. They are implemented using linked lists, while `Count` is an `O(N)` operation. If you need to check whether the collection is empty, use the `IsEmpty` property, which is an `O(1)` operation.

`ConcurrentDictionary` is a thread-safe dictionary collection implementation. It is lock free for read operations. However, it requires locking for write operations. The concurrent dictionary uses multiple locks, implementing a fine-grained locking model over the dictionary buckets. The number of locks could be defined by using a constructor with the parameter `concurrencyLevel`, which means that an estimated number of threads will update the dictionary concurrently.

Since a concurrent dictionary uses locking, there are a number of operations that require acquiring all the locks inside the dictionary. Please avoid using these operations without need. They are: `Count`, `IsEmpty`, `Keys`, `Values`, `CopyTo`, and `ToArray`.

`BlockingCollection` is an advanced wrapper over the `IProducerConsumerCollection` generic interface implementation. It has many features that are more advanced and is very useful to implement pipeline scenarios when you have some steps that use the results from processing the previous steps. The `BlockingCollection` class supports such features as blocking, bounding inner collections capacity, cancelling collection operations, and retrieving values from multiple blocking collections.

The concurrent algorithms can be very complicated, and covering all the concurrent collections—whether more or less advanced— would require writing a separate book. Here we illustrate only the simplest examples of using concurrent collections.

Using ConcurrentDictionary

This recipe shows a very simple scenario, comparing the performance of a usual dictionary collection with the concurrent dictionary in a single-threaded environment.

Getting ready

To work through this recipe, you will need Visual Studio 2012. There are no other prerequisites. The source code for this recipe can be found at `BookSamples\Chapter6\Recipe1`.

How to do it...

To understand the difference between performance of a usual dictionary collection with the concurrent dictionary, perform the following steps:

1. Start Visual Studio 2012. Create a new C# **Console Application** project.

2. In the `Program.cs` file add the following `using` directives:

```
using System;
using System.Collections.Concurrent;
using System.Collections.Generic;
using System.Diagnostics;
```

3. Add the following code snippet below the `Main` method:

```
const string Item = "Dictionary item";
public static string CurrentItem;
```

4. Add the following code snippet inside the `Main` method:

```
var concurrentDictionary = new ConcurrentDictionary<int,
    string>();
var dictionary = new Dictionary<int, string>();

var sw = new Stopwatch();

sw.Start();
for (int i = 0; i < 1000000; i++)
{
  lock (dictionary)
  {
    dictionary[i] = Item;
  }
}
```

```
    sw.Stop();
    Console.WriteLine("Writing to dictionary with a lock: {0}",
      sw.Elapsed);

    sw.Restart();
    for (int i = 0; i < 1000000; i++)
    {
      concurrentDictionary[i] = Item;
    }
    sw.Stop();
    Console.WriteLine("Writing to a concurrent dictionary:
      {0}", sw.Elapsed);

    sw.Restart();
    for (int i = 0; i < 1000000; i++)
    {
      lock (dictionary)
      {
        CurrentItem = dictionary[i];
      }
    }
    sw.Stop();
    Console.WriteLine("Reading from dictionary with a lock:
      {0}", sw.Elapsed);

    sw.Restart();
    for (int i = 0; i < 1000000; i++)
    {
      CurrentItem = concurrentDictionary[i];
    }
    sw.Stop();
    Console.WriteLine("Reading from a concurrent dictionary:
      {0}", sw.Elapsed);
```

5. Run the program.

How it works...

When the program starts, we create two collections. One of them is a standard dictionary collection and the other is a new concurrent dictionary. Then we start adding to it, using a standard dictionary with a lock and measuring the time it takes for one million iterations to complete. Then we measure the ConcurrentDictionary performance in the same scenario, and we finally compare the performance of retrieving values from both collections.

In this very simple scenario, we find that ConcurrentDictionary is significantly slower on write operations than a usual dictionary with a lock but is faster on retrieval operations. Therefore, if we need many thread-safe reads from a dictionary, the ConcurrendDictionary collection is the best choice.

If you need just read-only, multithreaded access to the dictionary, it may not be necessary to perform thread-safe reads. In this scenario, it is much better to use just a regular dictionary or the ReadOnlyDictionary collections.

ConcurrentDictionary is implemented using the **fine-grained locking** technique, and this allows it to scale better on multiple writes than using a regular dictionary with a lock (which is called **coarse-grained locking**). As we saw in this example, when we use just one thread, a concurrent dictionary is much slower, but when we scale this up to five-six threads (if we have enough CPU cores that could run them simultaneously), the concurrent dictionary will actually perform better.

Implementing asynchronous processing using ConcurrentQueue

This recipe will show an example of creating a set of tasks to be processed asynchronously by multiple workers.

Getting ready

To step through this recipe, you will need Visual Studio 2012. There are no other prerequisites. The source code for this recipe can be found in BookSamples\ Chapter6\Recipe2.

How to do it...

To understand the working of creating a set of tasks to be processed asynchronously by multiple workers, perform the following steps:

1. Start Visual Studio 2012. Create a new C# **Console Application** project.

2. In the Program.cs file add the following using directives:

```
using System;
using System.Collections.Concurrent;
using System.Threading;
using System.Threading.Tasks;
```

3. Add the following code snippet below the `Main` method:

```csharp
static async Task RunProgram()
{
  var taskQueue = new ConcurrentQueue<CustomTask>();
  var cts = new CancellationTokenSource();

  var taskSource = Task.Run(() => TaskProducer(taskQueue));

  Task[] processors = new Task[4];
  for (int i = 1; i <= 4; i++)
  {
    string processorId = i.ToString();
    processors[i-1] = Task.Run(
    () => TaskProcessor(taskQueue, "Processor " +
      processorId, cts.Token));
  }

  await taskSource;
  cts.CancelAfter(TimeSpan.FromSeconds(2));

  await Task.WhenAll(processors);
}

static async Task TaskProducer
  (ConcurrentQueue<CustomTask> queue)
{
  for (int i = 1; i <= 20; i++)
  {
    await Task.Delay(50);
    var workItem = new CustomTask {Id = i};
    queue.Enqueue(workItem);
    Console.WriteLine("Task {0} has been posted",
      workItem.Id);
  }
}

static async Task TaskProcessor(
  ConcurrentQueue<CustomTask> queue, string name,
  CancellationToken token)
{
  CustomTask workItem;
  bool dequeueSuccesful = false;

  await GetRandomDelay();
  do
  {
    dequeueSuccesful = queue.TryDequeue(out workItem);
    if (dequeueSuccesful)
    {
```

```
      Console.WriteLine("Task {0} has been processed by {1}",
        workItem.Id, name);
      }

      await GetRandomDelay();
    }
    while (!token.IsCancellationRequested);
  }

  static Task GetRandomDelay()
  {
    int delay = new Random(DateTime.Now.Millisecond).Next(1,
      500);
    return Task.Delay(delay);
  }

  class CustomTask
  {
    public int Id { get; set; }
  }
```

4. Add the following code snippet inside the `Main` method:

```
Task t = RunProgram();
t.Wait();
```

5. Run the program.

How it works...

When the program runs, we create a queue of tasks with an instance of the `ConcurrentQueue` collection. Then we create a cancellation token, which will be used to stop work after we are done posting tasks to the queue. Next, we start a separate worker thread that will be posting tasks to the tasks queue. This part produces a workload for our asynchronous processing.

Now let us define a task-consuming part of the program. We create four workers that will wait a random time, then get a task from the task queue, process it, and repeat the whole process until we signal the cancellation token. Finally, we start the task-producing thread, wait for its completion, and then signal to the consumers that we finished work with the cancellation token. The last step will be to wait for all our consumers to complete.

We see that we have tasks processing from start to end, but it is possible that a later task will be processed before an earlier one because we have four workers running independently and the task processing time is not constant. We see that the access to the queue is thread-safe; no work item was taken twice.

Changing asynchronous processing order ConcurrentStack

This recipe is a slight modification of the previous one. We will once again create a set of tasks to be processed asynchronously by multiple workers, but this time we implement it with `ConcurrentStack` and see the differences.

Getting ready

To step through this recipe, you will need Visual Studio 2012. There are no other prerequisites. The source code for this recipe can be found in `BookSamples\Chapter6\Recipe3`.

How to do it...

To understand the processing of a set of tasks implemented with `ConcurrentStack`, perform the following steps:

1. Start Visual Studio 2012. Create a new C# **Console Application** project.

2. In the `Program.cs` file add the following `using` directives:

   ```
   using System;
   using System.Collections.Concurrent;
   using System.Threading;
   using System.Threading.Tasks;
   ```

3. Add the following code snippet below the `Main` method:

   ```
   static async Task RunProgram()
   {
     var taskStack = new ConcurrentStack<CustomTask>();
     var cts = new CancellationTokenSource();

     var taskSource = Task.Run(() => TaskProducer(taskStack));

     Task[] processors = new Task[4];
     for (int i = 1; i <= 4; i++)
     {
       string processorId = i.ToString();
       processors[i - 1] = Task.Run(
       () => TaskProcessor(taskStack, "Processor " +
         processorId, cts.Token));
     }

     await taskSource;
     cts.CancelAfter(TimeSpan.FromSeconds(2));

     await Task.WhenAll(processors);
   ```

```
  }

  static async Task TaskProducer(ConcurrentStack<CustomTask>
    stack)
  {
    for (int i = 1; i <= 20; i++)
    {
      await Task.Delay(50);
      var workItem = new CustomTask { Id = i };
      stack.Push(workItem);
      Console.WriteLine("Task {0} has been posted",
        workItem.Id);
    }
  }

  static async Task TaskProcessor(
    ConcurrentStack<CustomTask> stack, string name,
      CancellationToken token)
  {
    await GetRandomDelay();
    do
    {
      CustomTask workItem;
      bool popSuccesful = stack.TryPop(out workItem);
      if (popSuccesful)
      {
      Console.WriteLine("Task {0} has been processed by {1}",
        workItem.Id, name);
      }

      await GetRandomDelay();
    }
    while (!token.IsCancellationRequested);
  }

  static Task GetRandomDelay()
  {
    int delay = new Random(DateTime.Now.Millisecond).Next(1,
      500);
    return Task.Delay(delay);
  }

  class CustomTask
  {
    public int Id { get; set; }
  }
```

4. Add the following code snippet inside the `Main` method:

```
Task t = RunProgram();
t.Wait();
```

5. Run the program.

How it works...

When the program runs, we now create an instance of the `ConcurrentStack` collection. The rest is almost like in the previous recipe, except instead of using the `Push` and `TryPop` methods on the concurrent stack, we use `Enqueue` and `TryDequeue` on a concurrent queue.

We now see that the task processing order has been changed. The stack is a LIFO collection and workers process the later tasks first. In case of a concurrent queue, tasks were processed in almost the same order in which they were added. This means that by depending on the number of workers, we will surely process the task that was created first in a given time frame. In case of a stack, the tasks that were created earlier will have lower priority and may be not processed until a producer stops putting more tasks to the stack. This behavior is very specific and it is much better to use a queue in this scenario.

Creating a scalable crawler with ConcurrentBag

This recipe shows how to scale workload between a number of independent workers that both produce work and process it.

Getting ready

To step through this recipe, you will need Visual Studio 2012. There are no other prerequisites. The source code for this recipe can be found in `BookSamples\Chapter6\Recipe4`.

How to do it...

The following steps demonstrate how to scale workload between a number of independent workers that both produce work and process it:

1. Start Visual Studio 2012. Create a new C# **Console Application** project.

2. In the `Program.cs` file add the following `using` directives:
   ```
   using System;
   using System.Collections.Concurrent;
   using System.Collections.Generic;
   using System.Threading.Tasks;
   ```

3. Add the following code snippet below the `Main` method:

```
static Dictionary<string, string[]> _contentEmulation = new
  Dictionary<string, string[]>();

static async Task RunProgram()
{
  var bag = new ConcurrentBag<CrawlingTask>();

  string[] urls = new[] {"http://microsoft.com/",
    "http://google.com/", "http://facebook.com/",
    "http://twitter.com/"};

  var crawlers = new Task[4];
  for (int i = 1; i <= 4; i++)
  {
    string crawlerName = "Crawler " + i.ToString();
    bag.Add(new CrawlingTask { UrlToCrawl = urls[i-1],
      ProducerName = "root"});
    crawlers[i - 1] = Task.Run(() => Crawl(bag,
      crawlerName));
  }

  await Task.WhenAll(crawlers);
}

static async Task Crawl(ConcurrentBag<CrawlingTask> bag,
  string crawlerName)
{
  CrawlingTask task;
  while (bag.TryTake(out task))
  {
    IEnumerable<string> urls = await
      GetLinksFromContent(task);
    if (urls != null)
    {
      foreach (var url in urls)
      {
        var t = new CrawlingTask
        {
          UrlToCrawl = url,
          ProducerName = crawlerName
        };

        bag.Add(t);
      }
    }
```

```
        Console.WriteLine("Indexing url {0} posted by {1} is
          completed by {2}!",
            task.UrlToCrawl, task.ProducerName, crawlerName);
      }
    }

    static async Task<IEnumerable<string>>
      GetLinksFromContent(CrawlingTask task)
    {
      await GetRandomDelay();

      if (_contentEmulation.ContainsKey(task.UrlToCrawl))
        return _contentEmulation[task.UrlToCrawl];

      return null;
    }

    static void CreateLinks()
    {
      _contentEmulation["http://microsoft.com/"] = new [] {
        "http://microsoft.com/a.html",
        "http://microsoft.com/b.html" };
      _contentEmulation["http://microsoft.com/a.html"] = new[]
        { "http://microsoft.com/c.html",
        "http://microsoft.com/d.html" };
      _contentEmulation["http://microsoft.com/b.html"] = new[]
        { "http://microsoft.com/e.html" };

      _contentEmulation["http://google.com/"] = new[] {
        "http://google.com/a.html", "http://google.com/b.html"
        };
      _contentEmulation["http://google.com/a.html"] = new[] {
        "http://google.com/c.html", "http://google.com/d.html"
        };
      _contentEmulation["http://google.com/b.html"] = new[] {
        "http://google.com/e.html", "http://google.com/f.html"
        };
      _contentEmulation["http://google.com/c.html"] = new[] {
        "http://google.com/h.html", "http://google.com/i.html"
        };

      _contentEmulation["http://facebook.com/"] = new [] {
        "http://facebook.com/a.html",
        "http://facebook.com/b.html" };
      _contentEmulation["http://facebook.com/a.html"] = new[] {
        "http://facebook.com/c.html",
        "http://facebook.com/d.html" };
      _contentEmulation["http://facebook.com/b.html"] = new[] {
        "http://facebook.com/e.html" };
```

```
  _contentEmulation["http://twitter.com/"] = new[] {
     "http://twitter.com/a.html",
     "http://twitter.com/b.html" };
  _contentEmulation["http://twitter.com/a.html"] = new[] {
     "http://twitter.com/c.html",
     "http://twitter.com/d.html" };
  _contentEmulation["http://twitter.com/b.html"] = new[] {
     "http://twitter.com/e.html" };
  _contentEmulation["http://twitter.com/c.html"] = new[] {
     "http://twitter.com/f.html",
     "http://twitter.com/g.html" };
  _contentEmulation["http://twitter.com/d.html"] = new[] {
     "http://twitter.com/h.html" };
  _contentEmulation["http://twitter.com/e.html"] = new[] {
     "http://twitter.com/i.html" };
}

static Task GetRandomDelay()
{
  int delay = new Random(DateTime.Now.Millisecond)
    .Next(150, 200);
  return Task.Delay(delay);
}

class CrawlingTask
{
  public string UrlToCrawl { get; set; }

  public string ProducerName { get; set; }
}
```

4. Add the following code snippet inside the `Main` method:

```
CreateLinks();
Task t = RunProgram();
t.Wait();
```

5. Run the program.

How it works...

The program simulates web-page indexing with multiple web crawlers. A web crawler is a program that opens a web page by its address, indexes the content, and tries to visit all the links that this page contains and index these linked pages as well. At the beginning, we define a dictionary containing different web-page URLs. This dictionary simulates web pages containing links to other pages. The implementation is very naive; it does not care about indexing already visited pages, but it is simple and allows us to focus on the concurrent workload.

Then we create a concurrent bag, containing crawling tasks. We create four crawlers and provide a different site root URL to each of them. Then we wait for all crawlers to compete. Now, each crawler starts to index the site URL it was given. We simulate the network I/O process by waiting for some random amount of time; then if the page contains more URLs, the crawler posts more crawling tasks to the bag. Then, it checks whether there are any tasks left to crawl in the bag. If not, the crawler completes.

If we check the output in the first lines below the first four, which were root URLs, we will see that usually a task posted by crawler number *N* is processed by the same crawler. However, the later lines will be different. This happens because internally `ConcurrentBag` is optimized for exactly this scenario where there are multiple threads that both add items and remove them. This is achieved by letting each thread work with its own local queue of items, and thus, we do not need any locks while this queue is occupied. Only when we have no items left in the local queue will we perform some locking and try to "steal" the work from another thread's local queue. This behavior helps to distribute the work between all workers and avoid locking.

Generalizing asynchronous processing with BlockingCollection

This recipe will describe how to use `BlockingCollection` to simplify implementation of workload asynchronous processing.

Getting ready

To step through this recipe, you will need Visual Studio 2012. No other prerequisites are required. The source code for this recipe can be found in `BookSamples\Chapter6\Recipe5`.

How to do it...

To understand how `BlockingCollection` simplifies the implementation of workload asynchronous processing, perform the following steps:

1. Start Visual Studio 2012. Create a new C# **Console Application** project.

2. In the `Program.cs` file add the following `using` directives:

```
using System;
using System.Collections.Concurrent;
using System.Threading.Tasks;
```

3. Add the following code snippet below the `Main` method:

```
static async Task RunProgram
  (IProducerConsumerCollection<CustomTask> collection =
  null)
{
  var taskCollection = new
    BlockingCollection<CustomTask>();
  if (null != collection)
  taskCollection= new
    BlockingCollection<CustomTask>(collection);

  var taskSource = Task.Run(() =>
    TaskProducer(taskCollection));

  Task[] processors = new Task[4];
  for (int i = 1; i <= 4; i++)
  {
    string processorId = "Processor " + i;
    processors[i - 1] = Task.Run(
      () => TaskProcessor(taskCollection, processorId));
  }

  await taskSource;

  await Task.WhenAll(processors);
}

static async Task TaskProducer
  (BlockingCollection<CustomTask> collection)
{
  for (int i = 1; i <= 20; i++)
  {
    await Task.Delay(20);
    var workItem = new CustomTask { Id = i };
    collection.Add(workItem);
    Console.WriteLine("Task {0} have been posted",
    workItem.Id);
  }
  collection.CompleteAdding();
}

static async Task TaskProcessor(
  BlockingCollection<CustomTask> collection, string name)
{
  await GetRandomDelay();
  foreach (CustomTask item in
    collection.GetConsumingEnumerable())
  {
```

```
      Console.WriteLine("Task {0} have been processed by
      {1}", item.Id, name);
      await GetRandomDelay();
    }
}

static Task GetRandomDelay()
{
  int delay = new Random(DateTime.Now.Millisecond).Next(1,
    500);
  return Task.Delay(delay);
}

class CustomTask
{
  public int Id { get; set; }
}
```

4. Add the following code snippet inside the `Main` method:

```
Console.WriteLine("Using a Queue inside of
  BlockingCollection");
Console.WriteLine();
Task t = RunProgram();
t.Wait();

Console.WriteLine();
Console.WriteLine("Using a Stack inside of
  BlockingCollection");
Console.WriteLine();
t = RunProgram(new ConcurrentStack<CustomTask>());
t.Wait();
```

5. Run the program.

How it works...

Here we take exactly the first scenario, but now we use a `BlockingCollection` class that provides many useful benefits. First of all, we are able to change the way the tasks are stored inside the blocking collection. By default, it uses a `ConcurrentQueue` container, but we are able to use any collection that implements the `IProducerConsumerCollection` generic interface. To illustrate this, we run the program twice, using `ConcurrentStack` as the underlying collection the second time.

Workers get work items by iterating over the `GetConsumingEnumerable` method call result on a blocking collection. If there are no items inside the collection, the iterator will just block the worker thread until an item is posted to the collection. The cycle ends when the producer calls the `CompleteAdding` method on the collection. It signals that the work is done.

 It is very easy to make a mistake and just iterate over `BlockingCollection` as it implements `IEnumerable` itself. Do not forget to use `GetConsumingEnumerable`, or else you will just iterate over a "snapshot" of a collection and get completely unexpected program behavior.

The workload producer inserts the tasks into `BlockingCollection` and then calls the `CompleteAdding` method, which causes all the workers to complete. Now in the program output we see two result sequences illustrating the difference between the concurrent queue and stack collections.

7
Using PLINQ

In this chapter, we will review different parallel programming paradigms, such as task and data parallelism, and cover the basics of data parallelism and parallel LINQ queries. You will learn about:

- ▶ Using the Parallel class
- ▶ Parallelizing a LINQ query
- ▶ Tweaking the parameters of a PLINQ query
- ▶ Handling exceptions in a PLINQ query
- ▶ Managing data partitioning in a PLINQ query
- ▶ Creating a custom aggregator for a PLINQ query

Introduction

In the .NET Framework, there is a subset of libraries that is called the Parallel Framework, often referred to as **Parallel Framework Extensions** (**PFX**), which was the name of the very first version of these libraries. Parallel Framework was released with .NET Framework 4.0 and consists of three major parts:

- ▶ **Task Parallel Library** (**TPL**)
- ▶ Concurrent collections
- ▶ Parallel LINQ or PLINQ

Through this book, we learned how to run several tasks in parallel and synchronize them with one another. In fact, we partition our program into a set of tasks and have different threads running different tasks. This approach is called **task parallelism**, and we have only been learning about task parallelism so far.

Imagine that we have a program that performs some heavy calculations over a big set of data. The easiest way to parallelize this program is to partition this set of data into smaller chunks, run the calculations needed over these chunks of data in parallel, and then aggregate the results of these calculations. This programming model is called **data parallelism**.

Task parallelism has the lowest abstraction level. We define the program as a combination of tasks, explicitly defining how they combine. A program composed in that way could be very complex and detailed. Parallel operations are defined in different places in this program, and as it grows, the program becomes harder to understand and maintain. This way of making the program parallel is called **unstructured parallelism**. It is the price to pay if we have complex parallelization logic.

However, when we have simpler program logic, we could try to offload more parallelization details to the PFX libraries and the C# compiler. For example, we could say, "I would like to run those three methods in parallel and I do not care how exactly this parallelization happens; let the .NET infrastructure decide the details". This raises the abstraction level as we do not have to provide a detailed description of how exactly we are parallelizing this. This approach is referred to as **structured parallelism** since the parallelization is usually a sort of declaration and each case of parallelization is defined in exactly one place in the program.

 There could be an impression that unstructured parallelism is a bad practice and structured should be always used instead. I would like to emphasize that this is not true. Structured parallelism is indeed more maintainable, and preferred when possible, but it is a much less universal approach. In general, there are many situations when we simply are not able to use it and it is perfectly OK to use the TPL task parallelism in an unstructured manner.

The Task Parallel Library has a `Parallel` class, which provides APIs for structured parallelism. This is still a part of TPL, but we will review it in this chapter because it is a perfect example of transition from a lower abstraction level to a higher one. When we use the `Parallel` class APIs, we do not need to provide the details of how we partition our work. However, we still need to explicitly define how we make one single result from partitioned results.

PLINQ has the highest abstraction level. It automatically partitions data to chunks and decides whether we really need to parallelize the query or whether it will be more effective to use usual sequential query processing. Then the PLINQ infrastructure takes care of combining the partitioned results together. There are many options that programmers may tweak to optimize the query and achieve the best possible performance and result.

In this chapter we will cover the `Parallel` class API usage and many different PLINQ options, such as making a LINQ query parallel, setting up execution mode and tweaking the parallelism degree of a PLINQ query, dealing with query item order, and handling PLINQ exceptions. We will also learn how to manage data partitioning for PLINQ queries.

Using the Parallel class

This recipe shows how to use the `Parallel` class APIs. We will learn how to invoke methods in parallel, how to perform parallel loops, and tweak parallelization mechanics.

Getting ready

To work through this recipe, you will need Visual Studio 2012. There are no other prerequisites. The source code for this recipe can be found in `BookSamples\Chapter7\Recipe1`.

How to do it...

To invoke methods in parallel, perform parallel loops, and tweak parallelization mechanics by using the `Parallel` class, perform the given steps:

1. Start Visual Studio 2012. Create a new C# **Console Application** project.

2. In the `Program.cs` file add the following `using` directives:

```
using System;
using System.Linq;
using System.Threading;
using System.Threading.Tasks;
```

3. Add the following code snippet below the `Main` method:

```
static string EmulateProcessing(string taskName)
{
    Thread.Sleep(TimeSpan.FromMilliseconds(
        new Random(DateTime.Now.Millisecond).Next(250, 350)));
    Console.WriteLine("{0} task was processed on a thread id
        {1}",taskName, Thread.CurrentThread.ManagedThreadId);
    return taskName;
}
```

4. Add the following code snippet inside the `Main` method:

```
Parallel.Invoke(
    () => EmulateProcessing("Task1"),
    () => EmulateProcessing("Task2"),
    () => EmulateProcessing("Task3")
);

var cts = new CancellationTokenSource();
```

```
var result = Parallel.ForEach(
  Enumerable.Range(1, 30),
  new ParallelOptions
  {
    CancellationToken = cts.Token,
    MaxDegreeOfParallelism = Environment.ProcessorCount,
    TaskScheduler = TaskScheduler.Default
  },
  (i, state) =>
  {
    Console.WriteLine(i);
    if (i == 20)
    {
      state.Break();
      Console.WriteLine("Loop is stopped: {0}",
        state.IsStopped);
    }
  });

Console.WriteLine("---");
Console.WriteLine("IsCompleted: {0}", result.IsCompleted);
Console.WriteLine("Lowest break iteration: {0}",
  result.LowestBreakIteration);
```

5. Run the program.

How it works...

This program demonstrates different features of the `Parallel` class. The `Invoke` method allows us to run several actions in parallel without much trouble as compared to defining tasks in the Task Parallel Library. The `Invoke` method blocks the other thread until all the actions are complete, which is quite a common and a convenient scenario.

The next feature is parallel loops, which are defined with the `For` and `ForEach` methods. We will look closely at `ForEach` since it is very similar to `For`. What you can do about the parallel `ForEach` loop is process any `IEnumerable` collection in parallel by applying an action delegate to each collection item. We are able to provide several options, customizing parallelization behavior, and get a result that shows whether the loop completed successfully.

To tweak our parallel loop, we provide an instance of the `ParallelOptions` class to the `ForEach` method. This allows us to cancel the loop with `CancellationToken`, restrict the maximum parallelism degree (how many maximum operations can be run in parallel), and provide a custom `TaskScheduler` class to schedule action tasks with it. Actions could accept an additional `ParallelLoopState` parameter, which is useful for breaking the loop or for checking what happens with the loop right now.

There are two ways of stopping the parallel loop with this state. We could use either the `Break` or `Stop` methods. The `Stop` method tells the loop to stop processing any more work, and sets the `IsStopped` property of the parallel loop state to `true`. The `Break` method stops the iterations after it, but the initial ones will continue to work. In that case, the `LowestBreakIteration` property of the loop result will contain a number of lowest loop iteration where the `Break` method was called.

Parallelizing a LINQ query

This recipe will describe how to use PLINQ to make a query parallel and how to go back from a parallel query to sequential processing.

Getting ready

To step through this recipe, you will need Visual Studio 2012. There are no other prerequisites. The source code for this recipe can be found in `BookSamples\Chapter7\Recipe2`.

How to do it...

To use PLINQ to make a query parallel and to go back from a parallel query to sequential processing, perform the following steps:

1. Start Visual Studio 2012. Create a new C# `Console Application` project.

2. In the `Program.cs` file add the following `using` directives:
```
using System;
using System.Collections.Generic;
using System.Diagnostics;
using System.Linq;
using System.Threading;
```

3. Add the following code snippet below the `Main` method:
```
static void PrintInfo(string typeName)
{
  Thread.Sleep(TimeSpan.FromMilliseconds(150));
  Console.WriteLine("{0} type was printed on a thread id
    {1}", typeName, Thread.CurrentThread.ManagedThreadId);
}

static string EmulateProcessing(string typeName)
{
  Thread.Sleep(TimeSpan.FromMilliseconds(150));
```

```
      Console.WriteLine("{0} type was processed on a thread id
         {1}",typeName, Thread.CurrentThread.ManagedThreadId);
      return typeName;
   }

   static IEnumerable<string> GetTypes()
   {
      return from assembly in
         AppDomain.CurrentDomain.GetAssemblies()
         from type in assembly.GetExportedTypes()
         where type.Name.StartsWith("Web")
         select type.Name;
   }
```

4. Add the following code snippet inside the `Main` method:

```
var sw = new Stopwatch();
sw.Start();
var query = from t in GetTypes()
   select EmulateProcessing(t);

foreach (string typeName in query)
{
   PrintInfo(typeName);
}
sw.Stop();
Console.WriteLine("---");
Console.WriteLine("Sequential LINQ query.");
Console.WriteLine("Time elapsed: {0}", sw.Elapsed);
Console.WriteLine("Press ENTER to continue....");
Console.ReadLine();
Console.Clear();
sw.Reset();

sw.Start();
var parallelQuery = from t in
   ParallelEnumerable.AsParallel(GetTypes())
   select EmulateProcessing(t);

foreach (string typeName in parallelQuery)
{
   PrintInfo(typeName);
}
sw.Stop();
Console.WriteLine("---");
```

```
Console.WriteLine("Parallel LINQ query. The results are
  being merged on a single thread");
Console.WriteLine("Time elapsed: {0}", sw.Elapsed);
Console.WriteLine("Press ENTER to continue....");
Console.ReadLine();
Console.Clear();
sw.Reset();

sw.Start();
parallelQuery = from t in GetTypes().AsParallel()
  select EmulateProcessing(t);

parallelQuery.ForAll(PrintInfo);

sw.Stop();
Console.WriteLine("---");
Console.WriteLine("Parallel LINQ query. The results are
  being processed in parallel");
Console.WriteLine("Time elapsed: {0}", sw.Elapsed);
Console.WriteLine("Press ENTER to continue....");
Console.ReadLine();
Console.Clear();
sw.Reset();

sw.Start();
query = from t in GetTypes().AsParallel().AsSequential()
  select EmulateProcessing(t);

foreach (var typeName in query)
{
   PrintInfo(typeName);
}

sw.Stop();
Console.WriteLine("---");
Console.WriteLine("Parallel LINQ query, transformed into
  sequential.");
Console.WriteLine("Time elapsed: {0}", sw.Elapsed);
Console.WriteLine("Press ENTER to continue....");
Console.ReadLine();
Console.Clear();
```

5. Run the program.

How it works...

When the program runs, we create a LINQ query that uses the reflection API to get all types whose names start with "Web" from the assemblies loaded in the current application domain. We emulate delays for processing each item and for printing it with the `EmulateProcessing` and `PrintInfo` methods. We also use the `Stopwatch` class to measure each query's execution time.

First we run a usual sequential LINQ query. There is no parallelization here, so everything runs on the current thread. The second version of the query uses the `ParallelEnumerable` class explicitly. `ParallelEnumerable` contains the PLINQ logic implementation and is organized as a number of extension methods to the `IEnumerable` collection's functionality. Normally we do not use this class explicitly; it is here to illustrate how PLINQ actually works. The second version runs `EmulateProcessing` in parallel; however, by default the results are being merged on a single thread, so the query execution time should be a couple of seconds less than the first version.

The third version shows how to use the `AsParallel` method to run the LINQ query in parallel in a declarative manner. We do not care about implementation details here but just state that we want to run this in parallel. However, the key difference in this version is that we use the `ForAll` method to print out the query results. It runs the action to all items in the query on the same thread they were processed in, skipping the results-merging step. It allows us to run `PrintInfo` in parallel as well, and this version runs even faster than the previous one.

The last sample shows how to turn a PLINQ query back to sequential with the `AsSequential` method. We can see that this query runs exactly like the first one.

Tweaking the parameters of a PLINQ query

This recipe shows how we can manage parallel processing options using a PLINQ query and what these options could affect during query execution.

Getting ready

To step through this recipe, you will need Visual Studio 2012. There are no other prerequisites. The source code for this recipe can be found in `BookSamples\Chapter7\Recipe3`.

How to do it...

To understand how to manage parallel processing options using a PLINQ query and their effects, perform the following steps:

1. Start Visual Studio 2012. Create a new C# **Console Application** project.

2. In the `Program.cs` file add the following `using` directives:

    ```
    using System;
    using System.Collections.Generic;
    using System.Linq;
    using System.Threading;
    ```

3. Add the following code snippet below the `Main` method:

    ```
    static string EmulateProcessing(string typeName)
    {
      Thread.Sleep(TimeSpan.FromMilliseconds(
        new Random(DateTime.Now.Millisecond).Next(250,350)));
      Console.WriteLine("{0} type was processed on a thread id
        {1}",typeName, Thread.CurrentThread.ManagedThreadId);
      return typeName;
    }

    static IEnumerable<string> GetTypes()
    {
      return from assembly in
        AppDomain.CurrentDomain.GetAssemblies()
        from type in assembly.GetExportedTypes()
        where type.Name.StartsWith("Web")
        orderby type.Name.Length
        select type.Name;
    }
    ```

4. Add the following code snippet inside the `Main` method:

```
var parallelQuery = from t in GetTypes().AsParallel()
  select EmulateProcessing(t);

var cts = new CancellationTokenSource();
cts.CancelAfter(TimeSpan.FromSeconds(3));

try
{
  parallelQuery.WithDegreeOfParallelism
    (Environment.ProcessorCount).WithExecutionMode
    (ParallelExecutionMode.ForceParallelism)
    .WithMergeOptions (ParallelMergeOptions.Default)
    .WithCancellation(cts.Token).ForAll(Console.WriteLine);
}
catch (OperationCanceledException)
{
  Console.WriteLine("---");
  Console.WriteLine("Operation has been canceled!");
}

Console.WriteLine("---");
Console.WriteLine("Unordered PLINQ query execution");
var unorderedQuery = from i in ParallelEnumerable.Range(1,
  30) select i;

foreach (var i in unorderedQuery)
{
  Console.WriteLine(i);
}

Console.WriteLine("---");
Console.WriteLine("Ordered PLINQ query execution");
var orderedQuery = from i in ParallelEnumerable.Range(1,
  30).AsOrdered() select i;

foreach (var i in orderedQuery)
{
  Console.WriteLine(i);
}
```

5. Run the program.

How it works...

The program demonstrates different useful PLINQ options that programmers can use. We start with creating a PLINQ query, and then we create another query providing PLINQ tweaking.

Let us start with cancellation first. To be able to cancel a PLINQ query, there is a `WithCancellation` method that accepts a cancellation token object. Here we signal the cancellation token after three seconds, which leads to `OperationCanceledException` in the query and cancellation of the rest of the work.

Then we are able to specify a parallelism degree for the query. It is the exact number of parallel partitions that will be used to execute the query. In the first recipe, we used the `Parallel.ForEach` loop, which has the maximum parallelism degree option. It is different because it specifies a maximum partitions value, but there could be fewer partitions if the infrastructure decides that it is better to use less parallelism to save resources and achieve optimal performance.

Another interesting option is overriding the query execution mode with the `WithExecutionMode` method. The PLINQ infrastructure can process some queries in sequential mode if it decides that parallelizing the query will only add more overhead and it actually will run slower. We can force the query to run in parallel.

To tune up query result processing we have the `WithMergeOptions` method. The default mode is to buffer a number of results selected by the PLINQ infrastructure before returning them from the query. If the query takes a significant amount of time, it is more reasonable to turn off the result buffering to get the results as soon as possible.

The last option is the `AsOrdered` method. It is possible that when we use parallel execution, the item order in the collection is not preserved. Later items in the collection could be processed before earlier ones. To prevent this we need to call `AsOrdered` on a parallel query to explicitly tell the PLINQ infrastructure that we intend to preserve item order for processing.

Handling exceptions in a PLINQ query

This recipe will describe how to handle exceptions in a PLINQ query.

Getting ready

To step through this recipe, you will need Visual Studio 2012. There are no other prerequisites. The source code for this recipe can be found in `BookSamples\Chapter7\Recipe4`.

How to do it...

To understand how to handle exceptions in a PLINQ query, perform the following steps:

1. Start Visual Studio 2012. Create a new C# **Console Application** project.

2. In the `Program.cs` file add the following `using` directives:

```
using System;
using System.Collections.Generic;
using System.Linq;
```

3. Add the following code snippet inside the `Main` method:

```
IEnumerable<int> numbers = Enumerable.Range(-5, 10);

var query = from number in numbers
  select 100 / number;

try
{
  foreach(var n in query)
    Console.WriteLine(n);
}
catch (DivideByZeroException)
{
  Console.WriteLine("Divided by zero!");
}

Console.WriteLine("---");
Console.WriteLine("Sequential LINQ query processing");
Console.WriteLine();

var parallelQuery = from number in numbers.AsParallel()
  select 100 / number;

try
{
  parallelQuery.ForAll(Console.WriteLine);
}
catch (DivideByZeroException)
{
  Console.WriteLine("Divided by zero - usual exception
    handler!");
}
catch (AggregateException e)
{
  e.Flatten().Handle(ex =>
  {
    if (ex is DivideByZeroException)
      {
```

```
            Console.WriteLine("Divided by zero - aggregate
              exception handler!");
            return true;
            }

        return false;
      });
    }

    Console.WriteLine("---");
    Console.WriteLine("Parallel LINQ query processing and
      results merging");
```

4. Run the program.

How it works...

First we run a usual LINQ query over a range of numbers from -5 to 4. When we divide by zero, we get `DivideByZeroException` and handle it as usual in a try/catch block.

However, when we use `AsParallel`, we will get `AggregateException` instead because we are now running in parallel, leveraging task infrastructure behind the scenes. `AggregateException` will contain all the exceptions that occurred while running the PLINQ query. To handle the inner `DivideByZeroException` class we use the `Flatten` and `Handle` methods, which were explained in the _Handling exceptions in asynchronous operations_ recipe in _Chapter 5, Using C# 5.0_.

 It is very easy to forget that when we handle aggregate exceptions, having more than one inner exception inside is a very common situation. If you forget to handle all of them, the exception will bubble up and the application will stop working.

Managing data partitioning in a PLINQ query

This recipe shows how to create a very basic custom partitioning strategy to parallelize a LINQ query in a specific way.

Getting ready

To step through this recipe, you will need Visual Studio 2012. There are no other prerequisites. The source code for this recipe can be found in `BookSamples\ Chapter7\Recipe5`.

How to do it...

To learn how to create a very basic custom partitioning strategy to parallelize a LINQ query, perform the following steps:

1. Start Visual Studio 2012. Create a new C# **Console Application** project.

2. In the `Program.cs` file add the following `using` directives:

```
using System;
using System.Collections.Concurrent;
using System.Collections.Generic;
using System.Linq;
using System.Threading;
```

3. Add the following code snippet below the `Main` method:

```
static void PrintInfo(string typeName)
{
  Thread.Sleep(TimeSpan.FromMilliseconds(150));
  Console.WriteLine("{0} type was printed on a thread id
    {1}",typeName, Thread.CurrentThread.ManagedThreadId);
}

static string EmulateProcessing(string typeName)
{
  Thread.Sleep(TimeSpan.FromMilliseconds(150));
  Console.WriteLine("{0} type was processed on a thread id
    {1}. Has {2} length.",typeName,
    Thread.CurrentThread.ManagedThreadId, typeName.Length %
    2 == 0 ? "even" : "odd");
  return typeName;
}

static IEnumerable<string> GetTypes()
{
  var types = AppDomain.CurrentDomain
    .GetAssemblies()
    .SelectMany(a => a.GetExportedTypes());

  return from type in types where
    type.Name.StartsWith("Web")
    select type.Name;
}

public class StringPartitioner : Partitioner<string>
{
```

```
   private readonly IEnumerable<string> _data;

   public StringPartitioner(IEnumerable<string> data)
   {
     _data = data;
   }

   public override bool SupportsDynamicPartitions
   {
     get
     {
      return false;
     }
   }

   public override IList<IEnumerator<string>>
     GetPartitions(int partitionCount)
   {
     var result = new List<IEnumerator<string>>(2);
     result.Add(CreateEnumerator(true));
     result.Add(CreateEnumerator(false));

     return result;
   }

   IEnumerator<string> CreateEnumerator(bool isEven)
   {
     foreach (var d in _data)
     {
       if (!(d.Length % 2 == 0 ^ isEven))
       yield return d;
     }
   }
}
```

4. Add the following code snippet inside the `Main` method:

```
var partitioner = new StringPartitioner(GetTypes());
var parallelQuery = from t in partitioner.AsParallel()
  select EmulateProcessing(t);

parallelQuery.ForAll(PrintInfo);
```

5. Run the program.

How it works...

To illustrate that we are able to choose custom partitioning strategies for the PLINQ query, we have created a very simple partitioner that processes strings of odd and even lengths in parallel. To achieve this we derive our custom `StringPartitioner` class from a standard base class `Partitioner<T>` using `string` as a type parameter.

We declare that we only support static partitioning by overriding the `SupportsDynamicPartitions` property and setting it to `false`. This means that we predefine our partitioning strategy. This is an easy way to partition the initial collection but could be inefficient depending on what data we have inside the collection. For example, in our case if we had many strings with odd lengths and only one string with even length, one of the threads will finish early and will not help to process odd-length strings. On the other hand, dynamic partitioning means that we partition the initial collection on the fly, balancing the work load between the worker threads.

Then we implement the `GetPartitions` method where we define two iterators. The first one returns strings with odd length from the source collection and the second one returns even-length strings. Finally, we create an instance of our partitioner and perform a PLINQ query with it. We can see that different threads process the odd- and even-length strings.

Creating a custom aggregator for a PLINQ query

This recipe shows how to create a custom aggregation function for a PLINQ query.

Getting ready

To step through this recipe, you will need Visual Studio 2012. There are no other prerequisites. The source code for this recipe can be found in `BookSamples\Chapter7\Recipe6`.

How to do it...

To understand the workings of custom aggregation function for a PLINQ query, perform the following steps:

1. Start Visual Studio 2012. Create a new C# **Console Application** project.

2. In the `Program.cs` file add the following `using` directives:

```
using System;
using System.Collections.Concurrent;
using System.Collections.Generic;
using System.Linq;
using System.Threading;
```

3. Add the following code snippet below the `Main` method:

```
static ConcurrentDictionary<char, int>
  AccumulateLettersInformation(ConcurrentDictionary<char,
    int> taskTotal , string item)
{
  foreach (var c in item)
  {
    if (taskTotal.ContainsKey(c))
    {
      taskTotal[c] = taskTotal[c] + 1;
    }
    else
    {
      taskTotal[c] = 1;
    }
  }
  Console.WriteLine("{0} type was aggregated on a thread id
    {1}",item, Thread.CurrentThread.ManagedThreadId);
  return taskTotal;
}

static ConcurrentDictionary<char, int>
  MergeAccumulators(ConcurrentDictionary<char, int> total,
  ConcurrentDictionary<char, int> taskTotal)
{
  foreach (var key in taskTotal.Keys)
  {
    if (total.ContainsKey(key))
    {
      total[key] = total[key] + taskTotal[key];
    }
    else
    {
      total[key] = taskTotal[key];
    }
  }
  Console.WriteLine("---");
  Console.WriteLine("Total aggregate value was calculated
    on a thread id {0}",
    Thread.CurrentThread.ManagedThreadId);
  return total;
}
```

```
static IEnumerable<string> GetTypes()
{
  var types = AppDomain.CurrentDomain
    .GetAssemblies()
    .SelectMany(a => a.GetExportedTypes());

  return from type in types
    where type.Name.StartsWith("Web")
    select type.Name;
}
```

4. Add the following code snippet inside the `Main` method:

```
var parallelQuery = from t in GetTypes().AsParallel()
  select t;

var parallelAggregator = parallelQuery.Aggregate(
  () => new ConcurrentDictionary<char, int>(),
  (taskTotal, item) => AccumulateLettersInformation
  (taskTotal, item),
  (total, taskTotal) => MergeAccumulators(total,
  taskTotal), total => total);

Console.WriteLine();
Console.WriteLine("There were the following letters in type
  names:");
var orderedKeys = from k in parallelAggregator.Keys
  orderby parallelAggregator[k] descending
  select k;

foreach (var c in orderedKeys)
{
  Console.WriteLine("Letter '{0}' ---- {1} times", c,
    parallelAggregator[c]);
}
```

5. Run the program.

How it works...

Here we implement custom aggregation mechanics that are able to work with the PLINQ queries. To implement this we have to understand that since a query is being processed in parallel by several tasks simultaneously, we need to provide mechanics to aggregate each task's result in parallel and then combine those aggregated values into one single result value.

In this recipe, we wrote an aggregating function that counts letters in a PLINQ query, which returns the IEnumerable<string> collection. It counts all the letters in each collection item. To illustrate the parallel aggregation process, we print out information about which thread processes each part of the aggregation.

We aggregate the PLINQ query results using the Aggregate extension method defined in the ParallelEnumerable class. It accepts four parameters, each of which is a function that performs different parts of the aggregation process. The first one is a factory that constructs the empty initial value of the aggregator. It is also called the seed value.

Please note that the first value provided to the Aggregate method is actually not an initial seed value for the aggregator function but a factory method that constructs this initial seed value. If you provide just an instance, it will be used in all partitions that run in parallel, which will lead to an incorrect result.

The second function aggregates each collection item into the partition aggregation object. We implement this function with the AccumulateLettersInformation method. It iterates over the string and counts the letters inside it. Here the aggregation objects are different for each query partition running in parallel, which is why we called them taskTotal.

The third function is a higher-level aggregation function that takes an aggregator object from a partition and merges it into a global aggregator object. We implement it with the MergeAccumulators method. The last function is a selector function that specifies what exact data we need from the global aggregator object.

Finally, we print out the aggregation result, ordering it by letters used most often in the collection items.

8
Reactive Extensions

In this chapter we will look at another interesting .NET library that helps us create asynchronous programs, the Reactive Extensions (or Rx). You will learn the following recipes:

- ▶ Converting a collection to asynchronous `Observable`
- ▶ Writing custom `Observable`
- ▶ Using `Subjects`
- ▶ Creating an `Observables` object
- ▶ Using LINQ queries against an `Observable` collection
- ▶ Creating asynchronous operations with Rx

Introduction

As we have already learned, there are several approaches to create asynchronous programs in .NET and C#. One of them is event-based asynchronous pattern, which was already mentioned in the previous chapters. The initial goal of introducing events was to simplify implementation of the `Observer` design pattern. This pattern is common for implementing notifications between objects.

When we discussed the Task Parallel Library, we noticed that the event's main shortcoming is their inability to be effectively composed with each other. The other drawback is that the Event-based Asynchronous Pattern is not supposed to be used to deal with the sequence of notifications. Imagine that we have `IEnumerable<string>` that gives us string values. However, when we iterate over it, we do not know how much time one iteration will take. It could be slow, and if we use the regular `foreach` or other synchronous iteration constructs, we will block our thread until we have the next value. This situation is called the **pull-based** approach when we as a client pull values from the producer.

The opposite approach is the **push-based** approach when the producer notifies the client about new values. This allows offloading the work to the producer, while the client is free to do anything else in the time it waits for another value. Therefore, the goal is to get something like the asynchronous version of `IEnumerable`, which produces a sequence of values and notifies the consumer about each item in the sequence, when the sequence completes, or when an exception has been thrown.

The .NET Framework starting from version 4.0 contains the definition of the interfaces `IObservable<out T>` and `IObserver<in T>` that together represent the asynchronous push-based collection and its client. They are coming from the library called Reactive Extensions (or simply Rx) that was created inside Microsoft to help effectively compose the sequence of events and actually all other types of asynchronous programs using the observable collections. The interfaces were included into the .Net Framework, but their implementations and all other mechanics are still distributed separately in the Rx library.

 Reactive Extensions is a cross-platform library in the first place. There are libraries for .NET 3.5, Silverlight, and Windows Phone. It is also available in JavaScript, Ruby, and Python. It is also open source; you can find Reactive extensions source code for .NET on the CodePlex website and other implementations on GitHub.

The most amazing thing is that the observable collections are compatible with LINQ, and therefore, we are able to use declarative queries to transform and compose those collections in an asynchronous manner. This also makes it possible to use the extension methods to add functionality to the Rx programs the same way it is used in the usual LINQ providers. Reactive extensions also support transition from all asynchronous programming patterns (including the Asynchronous Programming Model, the Event-based Asynchronous Pattern, and the Task Parallel Library) to observable collections, and it supports its own way of running asynchronous operations, which is still quite similar to TPL.

The Reactive Extensions library is a very powerful and complex instrument, worthy of writing a separate book. In this chapter I would like to review the most useful scenario, that is, how to work with asynchronous event sequences effectively. We will observe key types of the Reactive Extensions framework, learn to create sequences and manipulate them in different ways, and finally, check how we could use Reactive Extensions to run asynchronous operations and manage their options.

Converting a collection to asynchronous Observable

This recipe walks through how to create an observable collection from an `Enumerable` class and how to process it asynchronously.

Getting ready

To step through this recipe, you will need Visual Studio 2012. No other prerequisites are required. The source code for this recipe can be found at `BookSamples\Chapter8\Recipe1`.

How to do it...

To understand how to create an observable collection from an `Enumerable` class and process it asynchronously, perform the following steps:

1. Start Visual Studio 2012. Create a new C# **Console Application** project.
2. Add reference to the **Reactive Extensions Main Library** NuGet package.
   1. Right-click on the **References** folder in the project and select the **Manage NuGet Packages...** menu option.

2. Now add your preferred reference to the **Reactive Extensions - Main Library** NuGet package. You can use search in the **Manage NuGet Packages** dialog, as shown in the following screenshot:

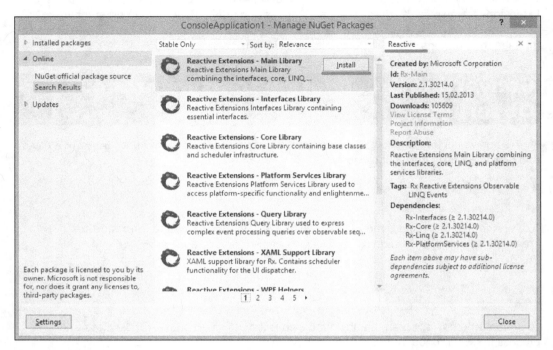

3. In the `Program.cs` file, add the following `using` directives:

```
using System;
using System.Collections.Generic;
using System.Reactive.Concurrency;
using System.Reactive.Linq;
using System.Threading;
```

4. Add the following code snippet below the `Main` method:

```
static IEnumerable<int> EnumerableEventSequence()
{
  for (int i = 0; i < 10; i++)
  {
    Thread.Sleep(TimeSpan.FromSeconds(0.5));
    yield return i;
  }
}
```

5. Add the following code snippet inside the `Main` method:

```
foreach (int i in EnumerableEventSequence())
{
  Console.Write(i);
}
Console.WriteLine();
Console.WriteLine("IEnumerable");

IObservable<int> o =
  EnumerableEventSequence().ToObservable();
using (IDisposable subscription =
  o.Subscribe(Console.Write))
{
  Console.WriteLine();
  Console.WriteLine("IObservable");
}

o = EnumerableEventSequence().ToObservable()
  .SubscribeOn(TaskPoolScheduler.Default);
using (IDisposable subscription =
  o.Subscribe(Console.Write))
{
  Console.WriteLine();
  Console.WriteLine("IObservable async");
  Console.ReadLine();
}
```

6. Run the program.

How it works...

We simulate a slow enumerable collection with the `EnumerableEventSequence` method. Then we iterate it in the usual `foreach` cycle and we can see that it is actually slow; we wait for each iteration to complete.

We then convert this enumerable collection to `Observable` with the help of the `ToObservable` extension method from the Reactive Extensions library. Next, we subscribe to the updates of this observable collection, providing the `Console.Write` method as the action, which will be executed on each update of the collection. As a result we get exactly the same behavior as before; we wait for each iteration to complete, because we use the main thread to subscribe to the updates.

We wrap the subscription objects into using statements. Although it is not always necessary, disposing off the subscriptions is a good practice that will avoid you lifetime-related bugs.

To make the program asynchronous, we use the `SubscribeOn` method providing it with the TPL task pool scheduler. This scheduler will place the subscription to the TPL task pool, offloading the work from the main thread. This allows us to keep the UI responsive and do something else, while the collection updates. To check this behavior, you could remove the last `Console.ReadLine` call from the code. When doing so we finish our main thread immediately, which forces all background threads (including the TPL task pool worker threads) to end as well, and we will get no output from the asynchronous collection.

If we are using any UI framework, we have to interact with the UI controls only from within the UI thread. To achieve this, we should use the `ObserveOn` method with the corresponding scheduler. For Windows Presentation Foundation, we have the `DispatcherScheduler` class and the `ObserveOnDispatcher` extension method defined in a separate NuGet package named Rx-XAML, or Reactive Extensions XAML support library. For other platforms there are corresponding separate NuGet packages as well.

Writing custom Observable

This recipe will describe how to implement the `IObservable<in T>` and `IObserver<out T>` interfaces to get the custom Observable sequence and properly consume it.

Getting ready

To step through this recipe, you will need Visual Studio 2012. No other prerequisites are required. The source code for this recipe can be found at `BookSamples\Chapter8\Recipe2`.

How to do it...

To understand implementing the `IObservable<in T>` and `IObserver<out T>` interfaces to get the custom Observable sequence and consume it, perform the following steps:

1. Start Visual Studio 2012. Create a new C# **Console Application** project.

2. Add reference to the **Reactive Extensions Main Library** NuGet package. Refer to the *Converting a collection to asynchronous observable* recipe, for details on how to do this.

3. In the `Program.cs` file, add the following `using` directives:

```
using System;
using System.Collections.Generic;
using System.Reactive.Concurrency;
using System.Reactive.Disposables;
using System.Reactive.Linq;
using System.Threading;
```

4. Add the following code snippet below the `Main` method:

```
class CustomObserver : IObserver<int>
{
  public void OnNext(int value)
  {
    Console.WriteLine("Next value: {0}; Thread Id: {1}",
      value, Thread.CurrentThread.ManagedThreadId);
  }

  public void OnError(Exception error)
  {
    Console.WriteLine("Error: {0}", error.Message);
  }

  public void OnCompleted()
  {
    Console.WriteLine("Completed");
  }
}

class CustomSequence : IObservable<int>
{
  private readonly IEnumerable<int> _numbers;

  public CustomSequence(IEnumerable<int> numbers)
  {
    _numbers = numbers;
  }
  public IDisposable Subscribe(IObserver<int> observer)
  {
    foreach (var number in _numbers)
    {
      observer.OnNext(number);
    }
    observer.OnCompleted();
    return Disposable.Empty;
  }
}
```

5. Add the following code snippet inside the `Main` method:

```
var observer = new CustomObserver();

var goodObservable = new CustomSequence(new[] {1, 2, 3, 4,
  5});
var badObservable = new CustomSequence(null);

using (IDisposable subscription =
  goodObservable.Subscribe(observer))
{
}

using (IDisposable subscription =
  goodObservable.SubscribeOn(TaskPoolScheduler.Default)
  .Subscribe(observer))
{
  Thread.Sleep(100);
}

using (IDisposable subscription =
  badObservable.SubscribeOn(TaskPoolScheduler.Default)
  .Subscribe(observer))
{
  Console.ReadLine();
}
```

6. Run the program.

How it works...

Here we implement our observer first, simply printing out to the console the information about the next item from the observable collection, error, or sequence completion. It is a very simple consumer code and there is nothing special about it.

The interesting part is our observable collection implementation. We accept an enumeration of numbers into a constructor, and do not check it for null on purpose. When we have a subscribing observer, we iterate over this collection and notify the observer about each item in the enumeration.

Then we demonstrate the actual subscription. As we can see, the asynchrony is achieved by calling the `SubscribeOn` method, which is an extension method to `IObservable` and contains asynchronous subscription logic. We do not care about asynchrony in our observable collection; we use standard implementation from the Reactive Extensions library.

When we subscribe to the normal observable collection, we just get all the items from it. It is now asynchronous, so we need to wait for some time for the asynchronous operation to complete, and only then print the message and wait for the user input.

Finally we try to subscribe to the next observable collection, where we are iterating over a null enumeration and therefore getting a null reference exception. We see that the exception has been properly handled and the `OnError` method was executed to print out the error details.

Using Subjects

This recipe shows how to use the Subject type family from the Reactive Extensions library.

Getting ready

To step through this recipe, you will need Visual Studio 2012. No other prerequisites are required. The source code for this recipe can be found at `BookSamples\Chapter8\Recipe3`.

How to do it...

To understand the use of the Subject type family from the Reactive Extensions library, perform the following steps:

1. Start Visual Studio 2012. Create a new C# **Console Application** project.

2. Add reference to **Reactive Extensions Main Library** NuGet package. Refer to the *Converting a collection to asynchronous observable* recipe for details on how to do this.

3. In the `Program.cs` file, add the following `using` directives:

    ```
    using System;
    using System.Reactive.Subjects;
    using System.Threading;
    ```

4. Add the following code snippet below the `Main` method:

    ```
    static IDisposable OutputToConsole<T>(IObservable<T> sequence)
    {
      return sequence.Subscribe(
        obj => Console.WriteLine("{0}", obj)
        , ex => Console.WriteLine("Error: {0}", ex.Message)
        , () => Console.WriteLine("Completed")
      );
    }
    ```

5. Add the following code snippet inside the `Main` method:

```
Console.WriteLine("Subject");
var subject = new Subject<string>();

subject.OnNext("A");
using (var subscription = OutputToConsole(subject))
{
  subject.OnNext("B");
  subject.OnNext("C");
  subject.OnNext("D");
  subject.OnCompleted();
  subject.OnNext("Will not be printed out");
}

Console.WriteLine("ReplaySubject");
var replaySubject = new ReplaySubject<string>();

replaySubject.OnNext("A");
using (var subscription = OutputToConsole(replaySubject))
{
  replaySubject.OnNext("B");
  replaySubject.OnNext("C");
  replaySubject.OnNext("D");
  replaySubject.OnCompleted();
}

Console.WriteLine("Buffered ReplaySubject");
var bufferedSubject = new ReplaySubject<string>(2);

bufferedSubject.OnNext("A");
bufferedSubject.OnNext("B");
bufferedSubject.OnNext("C");
using (var subscription = OutputToConsole(bufferedSubject))
{
  bufferedSubject.OnNext("D");
  bufferedSubject.OnCompleted();
}

Console.WriteLine("Time window ReplaySubject");
var timeSubject = new ReplaySubject<string>
  (TimeSpan.FromMilliseconds(200));

timeSubject.OnNext("A");
Thread.Sleep(TimeSpan.FromMilliseconds(100));
```

```
    timeSubject.OnNext("B");
    Thread.Sleep(TimeSpan.FromMilliseconds(100));
    timeSubject.OnNext("C");
    Thread.Sleep(TimeSpan.FromMilliseconds(100));
    using (var subscription = OutputToConsole(timeSubject))
    {
      Thread.Sleep(TimeSpan.FromMilliseconds(300));
      timeSubject.OnNext("D");
      timeSubject.OnCompleted();
    }

    Console.WriteLine("AsyncSubject");
    var asyncSubject = new AsyncSubject<string>();

    asyncSubject.OnNext("A");
    using (var subscription = OutputToConsole(asyncSubject))
    {
      asyncSubject.OnNext("B");
      asyncSubject.OnNext("C");
      asyncSubject.OnNext("D");
      asyncSubject.OnCompleted();
    }

    Console.WriteLine("BehaviorSubject");
    var behaviorSubject = new BehaviorSubject<string>
      ("Default");
    using (var subscription = OutputToConsole(behaviorSubject))
    {
      behaviorSubject.OnNext("B");
      behaviorSubject.OnNext("C");
      behaviorSubject.OnNext("D");
      behaviorSubject.OnCompleted();
    }
```

6. Run the program.

How it works...

In this program we look through different variants of a Subject type family. Subject represents both the IObservable and IObserver implementations. This is useful in different proxy scenarios when we want to translate events from multiple sources to one stream, or vice versa, to broadcast event sequence to multiple subscribers. Subjects are also very convenient for experimenting with Reactive Extensions.

Let's start with the basic Subject type. It retranslates event sequence to subscribers as soon as they subscribe to it. In our case, the A string will not be printed out because the subscription happened after it was transmitted. Besides that, when we call the `OnCompleted`, or `OnError` methods on `Observable`, it stops further translation of event sequence, so the last string will also not be printed out.

The next type, `ReplaySubject`, is quite flexible and allows us to implement three additional scenarios. First, it can cache all the events from the beginning of their broadcasting, and if we subscribe later, we will get all the preceding events first. This behavior is illustrated in the second example. Here, we shall have all four strings on the console, because the first event will be cached and translated to the latter subscriber.

Then we can specify the buffer size and the time window size for `ReplaySubject`. In the next example, we set the subject to have a buffer for two events. If more events are broadcasted, only the last two will be retranslated to the subscriber. So here we will not see the first string, because we have B and C in the subject buffer when subscribing to it. The same is the case with a time window. We can specify that the Subject caches only events that happened less than a certain time ago, discarding the older ones. Therefore, in the fourth example, we shall see only the last two events; the older events did not fit into the time-window limit.

`AsyncSubject` is something like a `Task` type from the Task Parallel Library. It represents a single asynchronous operation. If there are several events published, it waits for the event sequence completion and provides only the last event to the subscriber.

`BehaviorSubject` is quite similar to the `ReplaySubject` type, but it caches only one value and allows specifying a default value in case we did not send any notifications yet. In our last example, we shall see all the strings printed out, because we provided a default value, and all other events happened already after the subscription. If we move `behaviorSubject.OnNext("B");` line upwards below the `Default` event, it will replace the default value in the output.

Creating an Observable object

This recipe will describe different ways to create an `Observable` object.

Getting ready

To step through this recipe, you will need a running Visual Studio 2012. No other prerequisites are required. The source code for this recipe could be found at `BookSamples\Chapter8\Recipe4`.

How to do it...

To understand different ways of creating an `Observable` object, perform the following steps:

1. Start Visual Studio 2012. Create a new C# **Console Application** project.

2. Add reference to the **Reactive Extensions Main Library** NuGet package. Refer to the *Converting a collection to asynchronous Observable* recipe for details on how to do this.

3. In the `Program.cs` file, add the following `using` directives:

```
using System;
using System.Reactive.Disposables;
using System.Reactive.Linq;
using System.Threading;
```

4. Add the following code snippet below the `Main` method:

```
static IDisposable OutputToConsole<T>(IObservable<T> sequence)
{
  return sequence.Subscribe(
    obj => Console.WriteLine("{0}", obj)
    , ex => Console.WriteLine("Error: {0}", ex.Message)
    , () => Console.WriteLine("Completed")
  );
}
```

5. Add the following code snippet inside the `Main` method:

```
IObservable<int> o = Observable.Return(0);
using (var sub = OutputToConsole(o));
Console.WriteLine(" --------------- ");

o = Observable.Empty<int>();
using (var sub = OutputToConsole(o));
Console.WriteLine(" --------------- ");

o = Observable.Throw<int>(new Exception());
using (var sub = OutputToConsole(o));
Console.WriteLine(" --------------- ");

o = Observable.Repeat(42);
using (var sub = OutputToConsole(o.Take(5)));
Console.WriteLine(" --------------- ");
```

```
o = Observable.Range(0, 10);
using (var sub = OutputToConsole(o));
Console.WriteLine(" --------------- ");

o = Observable.Create<int>(ob => {
  for (int i = 0; i < 10; i++)
  {
    ob.OnNext(i);
  }
  return Disposable.Empty;
});
using (var sub = OutputToConsole(o)) ;
Console.WriteLine(" --------------- ");

o = Observable.Generate(
  0 // initial state
  , i => i < 5 // while this is true we continue the
  sequence
  , i => ++i // iteration
  , i => i*2 // selecting result
);
using (var sub = OutputToConsole(o));
Console.WriteLine(" --------------- ");

IObservable<long> ol =
  Observable.Interval(TimeSpan.FromSeconds(1));
using (var sub = OutputToConsole(ol))
{
  Thread.Sleep(TimeSpan.FromSeconds(3));
};
Console.WriteLine(" --------------- ");

ol = Observable.Timer(DateTimeOffset.Now.AddSeconds(2));
using (var sub = OutputToConsole(ol))
{
  Thread.Sleep(TimeSpan.FromSeconds(3));
};
Console.WriteLine(" --------------- ");
```

6. Run the program.

How it works...

Here, we walk through different scenarios of creating `observables`. Most of this functionality is provided as static factory methods of the `Observable` type. The first two samples show how we can create an `Observable` method that produces a single value and one that produces no value. In the next example we use `Observable.Throw` to construct an `Observable` class that triggers the `OnError` handler of its observers.

The `Observable.Repeat` method represents an endless sequence. There are different overloads of this method; here, we constructed an endless sequence by repeating 42 values. Then we use LINQ's `Take` method to take five elements from this sequence. `Observable.Range` represents a range of values, pretty much like `Enumerable.Range`.

The `Observable.Create` method supports more custom scenarios. There are a lot of overloads allowing us to use cancellation tokens and tasks, but let's look at the simplest one. It accepts a function, which accepts an instance of observer, and returns an `IDisposable` object representing a subscription. If we had any resources to cleanup, we would be able to provide the cleanup logic here, but we just return an empty disposable as we actually do not need it.

`Observable.Generate` is another way to create a custom sequence. We must provide an initial value for a sequence, then a predicate that determines if we should generate more items, or complete the sequence. Then we provide an iteration logic, which is incrementing a counter in our case. The last parameter is a selector function, allowing us to customize the results.

The last two methods deal with timers. `Observable.Interval` starts producing timer tick events with the `TimeSpan` period, and `Observable.Timer` specifies the startup time as well.

Using LINQ queries against the observable collection

This recipe shows how to use LINQ to query an asynchronous sequence of events.

Getting ready

To step through this recipe, you will need Visual Studio 2012. No other prerequisites are required. The source code for this recipe can be found at `BookSamples\Chapter8\Recipe5`.

How to do it...

To understand using LINQ queries against the observable collection, perform the following steps:

1. Start Visual Studio 2012. Create a new C# **Console Application** project.

2. Add reference to **Reactive Extensions Main Library** NuGet package. Refer to the *Converting a collection to asynchronous observable* recipe for details on how to do this.

3. In the `Program.cs` file, add the following `using` directives:

```
using System;
using System.Reactive.Linq;
```

4. Add the following code snippet below the `Main` method:

```
static IDisposable OutputToConsole<T>(IObservable<T> sequence,
int innerLevel)
{
  string delimiter = innerLevel == 0 ? string.Empty : new
    string('-', innerLevel*3);
  return sequence.Subscribe(
    obj => Console.WriteLine("{0}{1}", delimiter, obj)
    , ex => Console.WriteLine("Error: {0}", ex.Message)
    , () => Console.WriteLine("{0}Completed", delimiter)
  );
}
```

5. Add the following code snippet inside the `Main` method:

```
IObservable<long> sequence =
  Observable.Interval(TimeSpan.FromMilliseconds(50))
  .Take(21);

var evenNumbers = from n in sequence
  where n % 2 == 0
  select n;

var oddNumbers = from n in sequence
  where n % 2 != 0
  select n;

var combine = from n in evenNumbers.Concat(oddNumbers)
  select n;

var nums = (from n in combine
  where n % 5 == 0
  select n)
  .Do(n => Console.WriteLine("------Number {0} is processed
  in Do method", n));
```

```
using (var sub = OutputToConsole(sequence, 0))
using (var sub2 = OutputToConsole(combine, 1))
using (var sub3 = OutputToConsole(nums, 2))
{
  Console.WriteLine("Press enter to finish the demo");
  Console.ReadLine();
}
```

6. Run the program.

How it works...

The ability to use LINQ against the `Observable` event sequences is the main advantage of the Reactive Extensions framework. There are many different useful scenarios; unfortunately, it is impossible to show all of them here. I tried to provide a simple, yet very illustrative example, which does not have many complex details and shows the very essence of how a LINQ query could work when applied to asynchronous observable collections.

First, we create an `Observable` event that generates a sequence of numbers, one number every 50 milliseconds, and we start from the initial value of zero, taking twenty-one of those events. Then, we compose LINQ queries to this sequence. First, we select only the even numbers from the sequence, then only the odd numbers, and then we concatenate these two sequences.

The final query shows how to use a very useful method `Do`, which allows introducing side effects and, for example, logging each value from the resulting sequence. To run all queries, we create nested subscriptions, and because the sequences are initially asynchronous, we have to be very careful about the subscription's lifetime. The outer scope represents a subscription to the timer, the inner subscriptions deal with the combined sequence query and the side effects query, respectively. If we press *Enter* too early, we just unsubscribe from the timer and thus stop the demo.

When we run the demo, we see the actual process of how different queries interact in real time. We can see that our queries are lazy, and they start running only when we subscribe to their results. The timer events sequence is printed in the first column. When the even numbers query gets an even number, it prints it out as well using the - - - prefix to distinguish this sequence result from the first one. The final query results are printed to the right column.

When the program runs, we can see that the timer sequence, the even numbers sequence, and the side effect sequence are running in parallel. Only the concatenation waits until the even numbers sequence is complete. If we do not concatenate those sequences, we will have four parallel sequences of events interacting with each other in the most effective way! This shows the real power of Reactive Extensions, and could be a good start to learn this library in depth.

Creating asynchronous operations with Rx

This recipe shows how to create `Observable` from the asynchronous operations defined in other programming patterns.

Getting ready

To step through this recipe, you will need Visual Studio 2012. No other prerequisites are required. The source code for this recipe can be found at `BookSamples\Chapter8\Recipe6`.

How to do it...

To understand how to create asynchronous operations with Rx, perform the following steps:

1. Start Visual Studio 2012. Create a new C# **Console Application** project.

2. Add reference to **Reactive Extensions Main Library** NuGet package. Refer to the *Converting a collection to asynchronous observable* recipe for details on how to do this.

3. In the `Program.cs` file, add the following `using` directives:

```
using System;
using System.Reactive;
using System.Reactive.Linq;
using System.Reactive.Threading.Tasks;
using System.Threading;
using System.Threading.Tasks;
using System.Timers;
using Timer = System.Timers.Timer;
```

4. Add the following code snippet below the `Main` method:

```
static async Task<T> AwaitOnObservable<T>(IObservable<T>
  observable)
{
  T obj = await observable;
  Console.WriteLine("{0}", obj );
  return obj;
}

static Task<string> LongRunningOperationTaskAsync(string
  name)
{
  return Task.Run(() => LongRunningOperation(name));
}
```

```
static IObservable<string> LongRunningOperationAsync(string
  name)
{
  return Observable.Start(() =>
    LongRunningOperation(name));
}

static string LongRunningOperation(string name)
{
  Thread.Sleep(TimeSpan.FromSeconds(1));
  return string.Format("Task {0} is completed. Thread Id
    {1}", name, Thread.CurrentThread.ManagedThreadId);
}

static IDisposable OutputToConsole
  (IObservable<EventPattern<ElapsedEventArgs>> sequence)
{
  return sequence.Subscribe(
    obj => Console.WriteLine("{0}",
    obj.EventArgs.SignalTime)
    , ex => Console.WriteLine("Error: {0}", ex.Message)
    , () => Console.WriteLine("Completed")
  );
}

static IDisposable OutputToConsole<T>(IObservable<T>
  sequence)
{
  return sequence.Subscribe(
    obj => Console.WriteLine("{0}", obj)
    , ex => Console.WriteLine("Error: {0}", ex.Message)
    , () => Console.WriteLine("Completed")
  );
}
```

5. Add the following code snippet inside the `Main` method:

```
IObservable<string> o = LongRunningOperationAsync("Task1");
using (var sub = OutputToConsole(o))
{
  Thread.Sleep(TimeSpan.FromSeconds(2));
};
Console.WriteLine(" --------------- ");
```

```
Task<string> t = LongRunningOperationTaskAsync("Task2");
using (var sub = OutputToConsole(t.ToObservable()))
{
  Thread.Sleep(TimeSpan.FromSeconds(2));
};
Console.WriteLine(" --------------- ");

AsyncDelegate asyncMethod = LongRunningOperation;

// marked as obsolete, use tasks instead
Func<string, IObservable<string>> observableFactory =
  Observable.FromAsyncPattern<string, string>(
  asyncMethod.BeginInvoke, asyncMethod.EndInvoke);
o = observableFactory("Task3");
using (var sub = OutputToConsole(o))
{
  Thread.Sleep(TimeSpan.FromSeconds(2));
};
Console.WriteLine(" --------------- ");

o = observableFactory("Task4");
AwaitOnObservable(o).Wait();
Console.WriteLine(" --------------- ");

using (var timer = new Timer(1000))
{
  var ot = Observable.FromEventPattern<ElapsedEventHandler,
    ElapsedEventArgs>(
    h => timer.Elapsed += h
    ,h => timer.Elapsed -= h);
  timer.Start();

  using (var sub = OutputToConsole(ot))
  {
    Thread.Sleep(TimeSpan.FromSeconds(5));
  }
  Console.WriteLine(" --------------- ");
  timer.Stop();
}
```

6. Run the program.

How it works...

This recipe shows how to convert different types of asynchronous operations to an `Observable` class. The first code snippet in step 5 uses the `Observable.Start` method, which is quite similar to `Task.Run` from TPL. It starts an asynchronous operation that gives out a string result and then completes.

 I would strongly suggest using Task Parallel Library for asynchronous operations. Reactive Extensions supports this scenario as well, but to avoid ambiguity it is much better to stick with tasks when speaking about separate asynchronous operations and go with Rx only when we need to work with sequences of events. Another suggestion is to convert every type of separate asynchronous operation to tasks and only then convert a task to an `observable` class, if you need it.

Then, we do the same with tasks and convert a task to an `Observable` method by simply calling the `ToObservable` extension method. The next code snippet shown in step 5 is about converting Asynchronous Programming Model pattern to `Observable`. Normally, you would convert APM to a task, and then a task to `Observable`. However, there is a direct conversion, and this example illustrates how to run an asynchronous delegate and wrap it into an `Observable` operation.

The next part of the code snippet in step 5 shows that we are able to `await` an `Observable` operation. As we are not able to use the `async` modifier on an entry method such as `Main`, we introduce a separate method that returns a task and waits for this resulting task to complete inside the `Main` method.

The last part of this code snippet in step 5 is the same, but now we convert Event-based Asynchronous Pattern directly to an `Observable` class. We create a timer and consume its events for 5 seconds. We then dispose the timer to clean up the resources.

9
Using Asynchronous I/O

In this chapter, we will review asynchronous input/output operations in detail. You will learn the following:

- ► Working with files asynchronously
- ► Writing an asynchronous HTTP server and client
- ► Working with a database asynchronously
- ► Calling a WCF service asynchronously

Introduction

In the previous chapters, we already discussed how important it is to use asynchronous input/output operations properly. Why does it matter so much? To have a solid understanding, let us consider two kinds of applications.

If we run an application on the client, one of the most important things is to have a responsive user interface. This means that no matter what is happening with the application, all user interface elements, such as buttons and progress bars, keep running fast, and the user gets an immediate reaction from the application. This is not easy to achieve! If you try to open the notepad text editor in Windows and try to load a text document that is several megabytes in size, the application window will be frozen for a significant amount of time because the whole text is being loaded from the disk first, and only then the program starts to process user input.

This is an extremely important issue, and in this situation, the only solution is to avoid blocking the UI thread at all costs. This in turn means that to prevent blocking the UI thread, every UI-related API must allow only asynchronous calls. This is the key reason behind redesigning the APIs in the Windows 8 operating system by replacing almost every method with asynchronous analogs. But does it affect the performance if our application uses multiple threads to achieve this goal? Of course it does! However, we could pay the price considering that we have only one user. It is good if the application could use all the power of the computer to be more effective as all this power is intended for the single user who runs the application.

Let us look at the second case then. If we run the application on the server, we have a completely different situation. We have scalability as a top priority, which means that a single user should consume as little resource as possible. If we start to create many threads for each user, we simply cannot scale well. It is a very complex problem to balance our application resources consumption in an efficient way. For example, in ASP.NET, which is a web application platform from Microsoft, we use a pool of worker threads to serve clients' requests. This pool has a limited amount of worker threads, and we have to minimize the time of usage for each worker thread to achieve scalability. This means that we have to return it to the pool as soon as possible so that it could serve another request. If we start an asynchronous operation that requires computation, we will have a very inefficient workflow. First we take a worker thread from the thread pool to serve a client request. Then we take another worker thread and start an asynchronous operation on it. Now we have two worker threads serving our request, and it is good if the first thread is doing something useful! Unfortunately, the common situation is that we simply wait for the asynchronous operation to complete, and we consume two worker threads instead of one. In this scenario, asynchrony is actually worse than synchronous execution! We do not need to load all the CPU cores as we are already serving many clients and thus, are using all the CPU computing power. We do not need to keep the first thread responsive as we have no user interface. Then why should we use asynchrony in server applications?

The answer is that we should use asynchrony when there is an asynchronous input/output operation. Today, modern computers usually have a hard-disk drive that stores the files and a network card that sends and receives data over the network. Both of these devices have their own microcomputers that manage input/output operations on a very low level and signal the operating system about the results. This is again quite a complicated topic; but to keep the concept clear we could say that there is a way for the programmer to start an input/output operation and provide the operating system with a code to call back when the operation is completed. Between starting an I/O task and its completion, there is no CPU work involved; it is done in the corresponding disk and network-controller microcomputers. This way of executing an I/O task is called an I/O thread; they are implemented using the .NET thread pool and in turn use an infrastructure from the operating system called the I/O completion ports.

In ASP.NET, as soon as an asynchronous I/O operation is started from a worker thread, it can be returned immediately to the thread pool! While the operation is going on, this thread can serve other clients. Finally, when the operation signals completion, the ASP.NET infrastructure gets a free worker thread from the thread pool (which could be different from the one that started the operation), and it finishes the operation.

All right; we now understand how important I/O threads are for server applications. Unfortunately, it is very hard to see if any given API uses I/O threads under the hood. The only way besides studying the source code is simply to know which .NET Framework class library leverages the I/O threads. In this chapter, we will see how to use some of those APIs. We will learn how to work with files asynchronously, how to use network I/O to create an HTTP server and call Windows Communication Foundation service, and how to work with asynchronous API to query a database.

Another important issue to consider is parallelism. For a number of reasons, intensive parallel disk operation might have very poor performance. Please be aware that parallel I/O operations are often very ineffective, and it might be reasonable to work with I/O sequentially, but in an asynchronous manner.

Working with files asynchronously

This recipe walks us through how to create a file, and how to read and write data asynchronously.

Getting ready

To step through this recipe, you will need Visual Studio 2012. There are no other prerequisites. The source code for this recipe can be found at `BookSamples\Chapter9\Recipe1`.

How to do it...

To understand how to work with files asynchronously, perform the following steps:

1. Start Visual Studio 2012. Create a new C# **Console Application** project.

2. In the `Program.cs` file add the following `using` directives:

```
using System;
using System.IO;
using System.Linq;
using System.Text;
using System.Threading.Tasks;
```

3. Add the following code snippet below the `Main` method:

```
const int BUFFER_SIZE = 4096;

async static Task ProcessAsynchronousIO()
{
  using (var stream = new FileStream(
    "test1.txt", FileMode.Create, FileAccess.ReadWrite,
    FileShare.None, BUFFER_SIZE))
  {
    Console.WriteLine("1. Uses I/O Threads: {0}",
      stream.IsAsync);

    byte[] buffer = Encoding.UTF8.GetBytes
      (CreateFileContent());
```

```
    var writeTask = Task.Factory.FromAsync(
      stream.BeginWrite, stream.EndWrite, buffer, 0,
      buffer.Length, null);

    await writeTask;
}

using (var stream = new FileStream("test2.txt",
  FileMode.Create, FileAccess.ReadWrite,
  FileShare.None, BUFFER_SIZE, FileOptions.Asynchronous))
{
  Console.WriteLine("2. Uses I/O Threads: {0}",
    stream.IsAsync);

  byte[] buffer = Encoding.UTF8.GetBytes
    (CreateFileContent());
  var writeTask = Task.Factory.FromAsync(
    stream.BeginWrite, stream.EndWrite, buffer, 0,
    buffer.Length, null);

  await writeTask;
}

using (var stream = File.Create("test3.txt", BUFFER_SIZE,
  FileOptions.Asynchronous))
using (var sw = new StreamWriter(stream))
{
  Console.WriteLine("3. Uses I/O Threads: {0}",
    stream.IsAsync);
  await sw.WriteAsync(CreateFileContent());
}

using (var sw = new StreamWriter("test4.txt", true))
{
  Console.WriteLine("4. Uses I/O Threads: {0}",
    ((FileStream)sw.BaseStream).IsAsync);
  await sw.WriteAsync(CreateFileContent());
}

Console.WriteLine("Starting parsing files in parallel");

Task<long>[] readTasks = new Task<long>[4];
for (int i = 0; i < 4; i++)
{
  readTasks[i] = SumFileContent
    (string.Format("test{0}.txt", i + 1));
}

long[] sums = await Task.WhenAll(readTasks);
```

```csharp
      Console.WriteLine("Sum in all files: {0}", sums.Sum());

      Console.WriteLine("Deleting files...");

      Task[] deleteTasks = new Task[4];
      for (int i = 0; i < 4; i++)
      {
        string fileName = string.Format("test{0}.txt", i + 1);
        deleteTasks[i] = SimulateAsynchronousDelete(fileName);
      }

      await Task.WhenAll(deleteTasks);

      Console.WriteLine("Deleting complete.");
    }

    static string CreateFileContent()
    {
      var sb = new StringBuilder();
      for (int i = 0; i < 100000; i++)
      {
        sb.AppendFormat("{0}", new Random(i).Next(0, 99999));
        sb.AppendLine();
      }
      return sb.ToString();
    }

    async static Task<long> SumFileContent(string fileName)
    {
      using (var stream = new FileStream(fileName,
        FileMode.Open, FileAccess.Read,
        FileShare.None, BUFFER_SIZE, FileOptions.Asynchronous))
      using (var sr = new StreamReader(stream))
      {
        long sum = 0;
        while (sr.Peek() > -1)
        {
          string line = await sr.ReadLineAsync();
          sum += long.Parse(line);
        }

        return sum;
      }
    }

    static Task SimulateAsynchronousDelete(string fileName)
    {
      return Task.Run(() => File.Delete(fileName));
    }
```

4. Add the following code snippet inside the `Main` method:

```
var t = ProcessAsynchronousIO();
t.GetAwaiter().GetResult();
```

5. Run the program.

How it works...

When the program runs, we create four files in different manners and fill them up with random data. In the first case, we use the `FileStream` class and its methods, converting an Asynchronous Programming Model API to a task; in the second case, we do the same, but we provide `FileOptions.Asynchronous` to the `FileStream` constructor.

 It is very important to use the `FileOptions.Asynchronous` option. If we omit this option, we can still work with the file in an asynchronous manner, but this is just an asynchronous delegate invocation on a thread pool! We use the I/O asynchrony with the `FileStream` class only if we provide this option (or `bool useAsync` in another constructor overload).

The third case uses some simplifying APIs such as the `File.Create` method and the `StreamWriter` class. It still uses I/O threads, which we are able to check by using the `stream.IsAsync` property. The last case illustrates that oversimplifying is also bad. Here we do not leverage the I/O asynchrony by imitating it with the help of asynchronous delegate invocation.

Now we perform parallel asynchronous reading from files, summing their content, and then sum it with each other. Finally, we delete all the files. As there is no asynchronous delete file in any non-Windows store application, we simulate the asynchrony using the `Task.Run` factory method.

Writing an asynchronous HTTP server and client

This recipe shows how to create a simple asynchronous HTTP server.

Getting ready

To step through this recipe, you will need Visual Studio 2012. No other prerequisites are required. The source code for this recipe can be found at `BookSamples\Chapter9\Recipe2`.

How to do it...

The following steps demonstrate how to create a simple asynchronous HTTP server:

1. Start Visual Studio 2012. Create a new C# **Console Application** project.

2. Add a reference to the `System.Net.Http` framework library.

3. In the `Program.cs` file add the following `using` directives:

```
using System;
using System.IO;
using System.Net;
using System.Net.Http;
using System.Threading.Tasks;
```

4. Add the following code snippet below the `Main` method:

```
static async Task GetResponseAsync(string url)
{
  using (var client = new HttpClient())
  {
    HttpResponseMessage responseMessage = await
      client.GetAsync(url);
    string responseHeaders = responseMessage
      .Headers.ToString();
    string response = await responseMessage.Content
      .ReadAsStringAsync();

    Console.WriteLine("Response headers:");
    Console.WriteLine(responseHeaders);
    Console.WriteLine("Response body:");
    Console.WriteLine(response);
  }
}


class AsyncHttpServer
{
  readonly HttpListener _listener;
  const string RESPONSE_TEMPLATE =
    "<html><head><title>Test</title></head><body><h2>Test
    page</h2><h4>Today is: {0}</h4></body></html>";

  public AsyncHttpServer(int portNumber)
  {
    _listener = new HttpListener();
    _listener.Prefixes.Add(string.Format("http://+:{0}/",
      portNumber));
  }
```

```
public async Task Start()
{
  _listener.Start();

  while (true)
  {
    var ctx = await _listener.GetContextAsync();
    Console.WriteLine("Client connected...");
    string response = string.Format(RESPONSE_TEMPLATE,
      DateTime.Now);

    using (var sw = new StreamWriter
      (ctx.Response.OutputStream))
    {
      await sw.WriteAsync(response);
      await sw.FlushAsync();
    }
  }
}

public async Task Stop()
{
  _listener.Abort();
}
}
```

5. Add the following code snippet inside the `Main` method:

```
var server = new AsyncHttpServer(portNumber: 1234);
var t = Task.Run(() => server.Start());
Console.WriteLine("Listening on port 1234. Open
  http://localhost:1234 in your browser.");
Console.WriteLine("Trying to connect:");
Console.WriteLine();

GetResponseAsync("http://localhost:1234").GetAwaiter()
  .GetResult();

Console.WriteLine();
Console.WriteLine("Press Enter to stop the server.");
Console.ReadLine();

server.Stop().GetAwaiter().GetResult();
```

6. Run the program.

How it works...

Here we implement a very simple web server by using the `HttpListener` class. There is also a `TcpListener` class for the TCP socket I/O operations. We configure our listener to accept connections from any host to the local machine on port `1234`. Then we start the listener in a separate worker thread so that we can control it from the main thread.

The asynchronous I/O operation happens when we use the `GetContextAsync` method. Unfortunately, it does not accept `CancellationToken` for cancellation scenarios; so when we want to stop the server, we just call `_listener.Abort` method that abandons all the connection and stops the server.

To perform an asynchronous request to this server, we use the `HttpClient` class located in the `System.Net.Http` assembly and the same namespace. We use the `GetAsync` method to issue an asynchronous HTTP `GET` request. There are methods for the other HTTP requests such as `POST`, `DELETE`, and `PUT`. `HttpClient` has many other options such as serializing and deserializing an object using different formats such as XML and JSON, specifying a proxy server address, credentials, and others.

When you run the program, you can see that the server has been started up. In the server code, we use the `GetContextAsync` method to accept new client connections. This method returns when a new client connects, and we simply output a very basic HTML with the current date and time to the response. Then we request the server and print the response headers and content. You can also open your browser and browse to the `http://localhost:1234/` URL. You will see the same response displayed in the browser window.

Working with a database asynchronously

This recipe walks us through the process of creating a database, populating it with data, and reading data asynchronously.

Getting ready

To step through this recipe, you will need a running Visual Studio 2012. No other prerequisites are required. The source code for this recipe can be found at `BookSamples\Chapter9\Recipe3`.

How to do it...

To understand the process of creating a database, populating it with data, and reading data asynchronously, perform the following steps:

1. Start Visual Studio 2012. Create a new C# **Console Application** project.

2. In the `Program.cs` file add the following `using` directives:

```
using System;
using System.Data;
using System.Data.SqlClient;
using System.IO;
using System.Reflection;
using System.Threading.Tasks;
```

3. Add the following code snippet below the `Main` method:

```
async static Task ProcessAsynchronousIO(string dbName)
{
  try
  {
    const string connectionString = @"Data
      Source=(LocalDB)\v11.0;Initial
      Catalog=master;Integrated Security=True";
    string outputFolder = Path.GetDirectoryName
      (Assembly.GetExecutingAssembly().Location);
    string dbFileName = Path.Combine(outputFolder,
      string.Format(@".\{0}.mdf", dbName));
    string dbLogFileName = Path.Combine(outputFolder,
      string.Format(@".\{0}_log.ldf", dbName));
    string dbConnectionString = string.Format(@"Data
      Source=(LocalDB)\v11.0;AttachDBFileName={1};Initial
      Catalog={0};Integrated Security=True;", dbName,
      dbFileName);

    using (var connection = new SqlConnection
      (connectionString))
    {
      await connection.OpenAsync();

      if (File.Exists(dbFileName))
      {
        Console.WriteLine("Detaching the database...");

        var detachCommand = new SqlCommand("sp_detach_db",
          connection);
        detachCommand.CommandType = CommandType
          .StoredProcedure;
```

```
detachCommand.Parameters.AddWithValue("@dbname",
  dbName);

await detachCommand.ExecuteNonQueryAsync();

Console.WriteLine("The database was detached
  successfully.");
Console.WriteLine("Deleting the database...");

if(File.Exists(dbLogFileName)) File.Delete
  (dbLogFileName);
File.Delete(dbFileName);

Console.WriteLine("The database was deleted
  successfully.");
}

Console.WriteLine("Creating the database...");
string createCommand = String.Format("CREATE DATABASE
  {0} ON (NAME = N'{0}', FILENAME = '{1}')", dbName,
  dbFileName);
var cmd = new SqlCommand(createCommand, connection);

await cmd.ExecuteNonQueryAsync();
Console.WriteLine("The database was created
  successfully");
}

using (var connection = new SqlConnection(
  dbConnectionString))
{
  await connection.OpenAsync();

  var cmd = new SqlCommand("SELECT newid()",
    connection);
  var result = await cmd.ExecuteScalarAsync();

  Console.WriteLine("New GUID from DataBase: {0}",
    result);

  cmd = new SqlCommand(@"CREATE TABLE
    [dbo].[CustomTable]( [ID] [int] IDENTITY(1,1) NOT
    NULL, [Name] [nvarchar](50) NOT NULL,
    CONSTRAINT [PK_ID] PRIMARY KEY CLUSTERED ([ID] ASC)
    ON [PRIMARY]) ON [PRIMARY]", connection);
  await cmd.ExecuteNonQueryAsync();
```

```csharp
            Console.WriteLine("Table was created successfully.");

            cmd = new SqlCommand(@"INSERT INTO [dbo]
              .[CustomTable] (Name) VALUES ('John');
            INSERT INTO [dbo].[CustomTable] (Name) VALUES
              ('Peter');
            INSERT INTO [dbo].[CustomTable] (Name) VALUES
              ('James');
            INSERT INTO [dbo].[CustomTable] (Name) VALUES
              ('Eugene');", connection);
            await cmd.ExecuteNonQueryAsync();

            Console.WriteLine("Inserted data successfully  ");
            Console.WriteLine("Reading data from table...");

            cmd = new SqlCommand(@"SELECT * FROM [dbo]
              .[CustomTable]", connection);
            using (SqlDataReader reader = await
              cmd.ExecuteReaderAsync())
            {
              while (await reader.ReadAsync())
              {
                var id = reader.GetFieldValue<int>(0);
                var name = reader.GetFieldValue<string>(1);

                Console.WriteLine("Table row: Id {0}, Name {1}",
                  id, name);
              }
            }
          }
        }
        catch(Exception ex)
        {
          Console.WriteLine("Error: {0}", ex.Message);
        }
    }
```

4. Add the following code snippet inside the `Main` method:

```csharp
const string dataBaseName = "CustomDatabase";
var t = ProcessAsynchronousIO(dataBaseName);
t.GetAwaiter().GetResult();
Console.WriteLine("Press Enter to exit");
Console.ReadLine();
```

5. Run the program.

How it works...

This program works with a software called SQL Server 2012 LocalDb. It is installed with Visual Studio 2012 and should work fine. However in case of errors, you might want to repair this component from the installation wizard.

We start with configuring paths to our database files. We place database files in the program-execution folder. There will be two files: one for the database itself and another for the transaction log file. We also configure two connection strings that define how we connect to our databases. The first one is to connect to the LocalDb engine to detach our database; if it already exists, delete and then recreate it. We leverage the I/O asynchrony while opening the connection and while executing the SQL commands using the `OpenAsync` and `ExecuteNonQueryAsync` methods respectively.

After this task is complete, we are attaching a newly created database. Here we create a new table and insert a few data in it. In addition to the previously mentioned methods, we use `ExecuteScalarAsync` to asynchronously get a scalar value from the database engine, and we use the `SqlDataReader.ReadAsync` method to read a data row from the database table asynchronously.

If we had a large table with large binary values in its rows in our database, then we would use the `CommandBehavior.SequentialAcess` enumeration to create the data reader and the `GetFieldValueAsync` method to get large field values from the reader asynchronously.

Calling a WCF service asynchronously

This recipe will describe how to create a WCF service, host it in a console application, make service metadata available to clients, and how to consume it in an asynchronous way.

Getting ready

To step through this recipe, you will need a running Visual Studio 2012. There are no other prerequisites. The source code for this recipe can be found at `BookSamples\Chapter9\Recipe4`.

How to do it...

To understand how to work with a WCF service, perform the following steps:

1. Start Visual Studio 2012. Create a new C# **Console Application** project.

2. Add references to the `System.ServiceModel` library. Right-click on the `References` folder in the project and select the **Add reference...** menu option. Add references to the `System.ServiceModel` library. You can use the search function in the reference manager dialog as shown in the following screenshot:

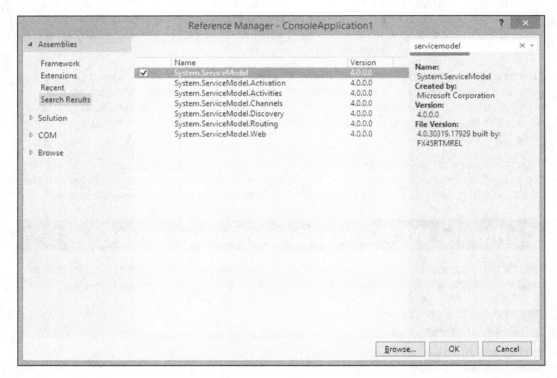

3. In the `Program.cs` file add the following `using` directives:

```
using System;
using System.ServiceModel;
using System.ServiceModel.Description;
using System.Threading.Tasks;
```

4. Add the following code snippet below the `Main` method:

```
const string SERVICE_URL =
  "http://localhost:1234/HelloWorld";

static async Task RunServiceClient()
{
  var endpoint = new EndpointAddress(SERVICE_URL);
  var channel = ChannelFactory
    <IHelloWorldServiceClient>.CreateChannel(new
    BasicHttpBinding(), endpoint);

  var greeting = await channel.GreetAsync("Eugene");
  Console.WriteLine(greeting);
}

  [ServiceContract(Namespace = "Packt", Name =
    "HelloWorldServiceContract")]
public interface IHelloWorldService
{
  [OperationContract]
  string Greet(string name);
}

[ServiceContract(Namespace = "Packt", Name =
  "HelloWorldServiceContract")]
public interface IHelloWorldServiceClient
{
  [OperationContract]
    string Greet(string name);

  [OperationContract]
    Task<string> GreetAsync(string name);
}

public class HelloWorldService : IHelloWorldService
{
  public string Greet(string name)
  {
    return string.Format("Greetings, {0}!", name);
  }
}
```

5. Add the following code snippet inside the `Main` method:

```
ServiceHost host = null;

try
{
  host = new ServiceHost(typeof (HelloWorldService), new
    Uri(SERVICE_URL));
  var metadata = host.Description.Behaviors.
    Find<ServiceMetadataBehavior>();
  if (null == metadata)
  {
    metadata = new ServiceMetadataBehavior();
  }

  metadata.HttpGetEnabled = true;
  metadata.MetadataExporter.PolicyVersion =
    PolicyVersion.Policy15;
  host.Description.Behaviors.Add(metadata);

  host.AddServiceEndpoint(ServiceMetadataBehavior
    .MexContractName, MetadataExchangeBindings
    .CreateMexHttpBinding(),"mex");
  var endpoint = host.AddServiceEndpoint(typeof
    (IHelloWorldService), new BasicHttpBinding(),
    SERVICE_URL);

  host.Faulted += (sender, e) =>
    Console.WriteLine("Error!");

  host.Open();

  Console.WriteLine("Greeting service is running and
    listening on:");
  Console.WriteLine("{0} ({1})", endpoint.Address,
    endpoint.Binding.Name);

  var client = RunServiceClient();
  client.GetAwaiter().GetResult();

  Console.WriteLine("Press Enter to exit");
  Console.ReadLine();
}
catch (Exception ex)
{
```

```
      Console.WriteLine("Error in catch block: {0}", ex);
    }
    finally
    {
      if (null != host)
      {
        if (host.State == CommunicationState.Faulted)
        {
          host.Abort();
        }
        else
        {
          host.Close();
        }
      }
    }
```

6. Run the program.

How it works...

Windows Communication Foundation or WCF is a framework that allows us to call remote services in different ways. One of them, which was very popular some time ago, was used to call remote services via HTTP using an XML-based protocol called **Simple Object Access Protocol (SOAP)**. It is quite common when a server application calls another remote service, and it could be done using I/O threads as well.

Visual Studio 2012 has rich support for WCF services; for example, you can add references to such services with the **Add Service Reference** menu option. You could do it with our service as well because we provide service metadata.

To create such a service we need to use a ServiceHost class that will be hosting our service. We describe what service we will be hosting by providing a service implementation type and the base URI by which the service would be addressed. Then we configure the metadata endpoint and the service endpoint. Finally, we handle the Faulted event in case of errors and run the host service.

To consume this service, we create a client, and here is where the main trick happens. On the server side, we have a service with the usual synchronous method called `Greet`. This method is defined in the service contract, `IHelloWorldService`. However, if we want to leverage an asynchronous network I/O, we have to call this method asynchronously. We can do that by creating a new service contract with matching namespace and service name, where we define both the synchronous and task-based asynchronous methods. In spite of the fact that we do not have an asynchronous method definition on a server side, we follow the naming convention, and the WCF infrastructure understands that we want to create an asynchronous proxy method.

Therefore, when we create an `IHelloWorldServiceClient` proxy channel, and WCF correctly routes an asynchronous call to the server-side synchronous method. If you leave the application running, you can open the browser and access the service using its URL that is `http://localhost:1234/HelloWorld`. There will be a service description opened, and you can browse to the XML metadata that allows us to add a service reference from Visual Studio 2012. If you try to generate the reference, you will see a slightly more complicated code, but it is autogenerated and easy to use.

10
Parallel Programming Patterns

In this chapter, we will review the common problems that a programmer often faces while trying to implement parallel workflow. You will learn about:

- ▸ Implementing Lazy-evaluated shared states
- ▸ Implementing Parallel Pipeline with BlockingCollection
- ▸ Implementing Parallel Pipeline with TPL DataFlow
- ▸ Implementing Map/Reduce with PLINQ

Introduction

Patterns in programming mean a concrete and standard solution to a given problem. Usually, programming patterns are the result of people gathering experience, analyzing the common problems, and providing solutions to these problems.

Since parallel programming has existed for quite a long time, there are many different patterns for programming parallel applications. There are even special programming languages to make programming of specific parallel algorithms easier. However, this is where things start to become increasingly complicated. In this book, I will provide a starting point from where you will be able to study parallel programming further. We will review very basic, yet very useful, patterns that are quite helpful for many common situations in parallel programming.

First is about using a **shared-state object** from multiple threads. I would like to emphasize that you should avoid it as much as possible. As we have discussed in previous chapters, shared state is really bad when you write parallel algorithms, but in many occasions it is inevitable. We will find out how to delay an actual computation of an object until it is needed, and how to implement different scenarios to achieve thread safety.

The next two recipes will show how to create a structured parallel data flow. We will review a concrete case of a producer/consumer pattern, which is called as **Parallel Pipeline**. We are going to implement it by just blocking the collection first, and then see how helpful is another library from Microsoft for parallel programming—**TPL DataFlow**.

The last pattern that we will study is the **Map/Reduce** pattern. In the modern world, this name could mean very different things. Some people consider map/reduce not as a common approach to any problem but as a concrete implementation for large, distributed cluster computations. We will find out the meaning behind the name of this pattern and review some examples of how it might work in case of small parallel applications.

Implementing Lazy-evaluated shared states

This recipe shows how to program a Lazy-evaluated thread-safe shared state object.

Getting ready

To start with this recipe, you will need a running Visual Studio 2012. There are no other prerequisites. The source code for this recipe can be found at `BookSamples\Chapter10\Recipe1`.

How to do it...

For implementing Lazy-evaluated shared states, perform the following steps:

1. Start Visual Studio 2012. Create a new C# **Console Application** project.

2. In the `Program.cs` file, add the following `using` directives:

```
using System;
using System.Threading;
using System.Threading.Tasks;
```

3. Add the following code snippet below the `Main` method:

```
static async Task ProcessAsynchronously()
{
  var unsafeState = new UnsafeState();
  Task[] tasks = new Task[4];

  for (int i = 0; i < 4; i++)
  {
    tasks[i] = Task.Run(() => Worker(unsafeState));
  }
  await Task.WhenAll(tasks);
  Console.WriteLine(" -------------------------- ");
```

```
    var firstState = new DoubleCheckedLocking();
    for (int i = 0; i < 4; i++)
    {
      tasks[i] = Task.Run(() => Worker(firstState));
    }

    await Task.WhenAll(tasks);
    Console.WriteLine(" ------------------------- ");

    var secondState = new BCLDoubleChecked();
    for (int i = 0; i < 4; i++)
    {
      tasks[i] = Task.Run(() => Worker(secondState));
    }

    await Task.WhenAll(tasks);
    Console.WriteLine(" ------------------------- ");

    var thirdState = new Lazy<ValueToAccess>(Compute);
    for (int i = 0; i < 4; i++)
    {
      tasks[i] = Task.Run(() => Worker(thirdState));
    }

    await Task.WhenAll(tasks);
    Console.WriteLine(" ------------------------- ");

    var fourthState = new BCLThreadSafeFactory();
    for (int i = 0; i < 4; i++)
    {
      tasks[i] = Task.Run(() => Worker(fourthState));
    }

    await Task.WhenAll(tasks);
    Console.WriteLine(" ------------------------- ");
  }

  static void Worker(IHasValue state)
  {
    Console.WriteLine("Worker runs on thread id {0}",
      Thread.CurrentThread.ManagedThreadId);
    Console.WriteLine("State value: {0}", state.Value.Text);
  }

  static void Worker(Lazy<ValueToAccess> state)
  {
    Console.WriteLine("Worker runs on thread id {0}",
      Thread.CurrentThread.ManagedThreadId);
    Console.WriteLine("State value: {0}", state.Value.Text);
```

```
      }

      static ValueToAccess Compute()
      {
        Console.WriteLine("The value is being constructed on a
          thread id {0}", Thread.CurrentThread.ManagedThreadId);
        Thread.Sleep(TimeSpan.FromSeconds(1));
        return new ValueToAccess(string.Format(
          "Constructed on thread id {0}",
            Thread.CurrentThread.ManagedThreadId));
      }

      class ValueToAccess
      {
        private readonly string _text;
        public ValueToAccess(string text)
        {
          _text = text;
        }

        public string Text
        {
          get { return _text; }
        }
      }

      class UnsafeState : IHasValue
      {
        private ValueToAccess _value;

        public ValueToAccess Value
        {
          get
          {
            if (_value == null)
            {
              _value = Compute();
            }
            return _value;
          }
        }


      }

      class DoubleCheckedLocking : IHasValue
      {
        private object _syncRoot = new object();
        private volatile ValueToAccess _value;

        public ValueToAccess Value
```

```
      {
        get
        {
          if (_value == null)
          {
            lock (_syncRoot)
            {
              if (_value == null) _value = Compute();
            }
          }
          return _value;
        }
      }
    }

    class BCLDoubleChecked : IHasValue
    {
      private object _syncRoot = new object();
      private ValueToAccess _value;
      private bool _initialized = false;

      public ValueToAccess Value
      {
        get
        {
          return LazyInitializer.EnsureInitialized(
            ref _value, ref _initialized, ref _syncRoot,
              Compute);
        }
      }
    }

    class BCLThreadSafeFactory : IHasValue
    {
      private ValueToAccess _value;

      public ValueToAccess Value
      {
        get
        {
          return LazyInitializer.EnsureInitialized(ref _value,
            Compute);
        }
      }
    }

    interface IHasValue
    {
      ValueToAccess Value { get; }
    }
```

4. Add the following code snippet inside the `Main` method:

```
var t = ProcessAsynchronously();
t.GetAwaiter().GetResult();

Console.WriteLine("Press ENTER to exit");
Console.ReadLine();
```

5. Run the program.

How it works...

The first example show why it is not safe to use the `UnsafeState` object with multiple accessing threads. We see that the `Construct` method was called several times, and different threads use different values, which is obviously not right. To fix this, we can use a lock when reading the value, and if it is not initialized, create it first. It will work, but using a lock with every read operation is not efficient. To avoid using locks every time, there is a traditional approach called the **double-checked locking** pattern. We check the value for the first time, and if is not null, we avoid unnecessary locking and just use the shared object. However, if it was not constructed yet, we use the lock and then check the value for the second time, because it could be initialized between our first check and the lock operation. If it is still not initialized, only then we compute the value. We can clearly see that this approach works with the second example—there is only one call to the `Construct` method, and the first-called thread defines the shared object state.

> Please note that if the lazy- evaluated object implementation is thread-safe, it does not automatically mean that all its properties are thread-safe as well.
>
> If you add, for example, an **int** public property to the `ValueToAccess` object, it will not be thread-safe; you still have to use interlocked constructs or locking to ensure thread safety.

This pattern is very common, and that is why there are several classes in the Base Class Library to help us. First, we can use the `LazyInitializer.EnsureInitialized` method, which implements the double-checked locking pattern inside. However, the most comfortable option is to use the `Lazy<T>` class that allows us to have thread-safe Lazy-evaluated, shared state, out of the box. The next two examples show us that they are equivalent to the second one, and the program behaves the same. The only difference is that since `LazyInitializer` is a static class, we do not have to create a new instance of a class as we do in the case of `Lazy<T>`, and therefore the performance in the first case will be better in some scenarios.

The last option is to avoid locking at all, if we do not care about the `Construct` method. If it is thread-safe and has no side effects and/or serious performance impacts, we can just run it several times but use only the first constructed value. The last example shows the described behavior, and we can achieve this result by using another `LazyInitializer`. `EnsureInitialized` method overload.

Implementing Parallel Pipeline with BlockingCollection

This recipe will describe how to implement a specific scenario of a producer/consumer pattern, which is called Parallel Pipeline, using the standard `BlockingCollection` data structure.

Getting ready

To begin this recipe, you will need a running Visual Studio 2012. There are no other prerequisites. The source code for this recipe can be found at `7644_Code\Chapter10\Recipe2`.

How to do it...

To understand how to implement Parallel Pipeline using `BlockingCollection`, perform the following steps:

1. Start Visual Studio 2012. Create a new C# **Console Application** project.

2. In the `Program.cs` file, add the following `using` directives:

```
using System;
using System.Collections.Concurrent;
using System.Linq;
using System.Threading;
using System.Threading.Tasks;
```

3. Add the following code snippet below the `Main` method:

```
private const int CollectionsNumber = 4;
private const int Count = 10;

class PipelineWorker<TInput, TOutput>
{
    Func<TInput, TOutput> _processor = null;
    Action<TInput> _outputProcessor = null;
    BlockingCollection<TInput>[] _input;
    CancellationToken _token;
```

```
        public PipelineWorker(
            BlockingCollection<TInput>[] input,
            Func<TInput, TOutput> processor,
            CancellationToken token,
            string name)
    {
      _input = input;
      Output = new BlockingCollection<TOutput>[_input.Length];
      for (int i = 0; i < Output.Length; i++)
          Output[i] = null == input[i] ? null : new BlockingCollection
  <TOutput>(Count);

        _processor = processor;
        _token = token;
        Name = name;
    }


    public PipelineWorker(
        BlockingCollection<TInput>[] input,
        Action<TInput> renderer,
        CancellationToken token,
        string name)
    {
      _input = input;
      _outputProcessor = renderer;
      _token = token;
      Name = name;
      Output = null;
    }


    public BlockingCollection<TOutput>[] Output { get; private set;
  }

    public string Name { get; private set; }

    public void Run()
    {
      Console.WriteLine("{0} is running", this.Name);
      while (!_input.All(bc => bc.IsCompleted) && !_token.
  IsCancellationRequested)
        {
          TInput receivedItem;
          int i = BlockingCollection<TInput>.TryTakeFromAny(
              _input, out receivedItem, 50, _token);
```

```
      if (i >= 0)
      {
        if (Output != null)
        {
          TOutput outputItem = _processor(receivedItem);
          BlockingCollection<TOutput>.AddToAny(Output,
            outputItem);
          Console.WriteLine("{0} sent {1} to next,
            on thread id {2}", Name, outputItem,
              Thread.CurrentThread.ManagedThreadId);
          Thread.Sleep(TimeSpan.FromMilliseconds(100));
        }
        else
        {
          _outputProcessor(receivedItem);
        }
      }
      else
      {
        Thread.Sleep(TimeSpan.FromMilliseconds(50));
      }
    }
    if (Output != null)
    {
      foreach (var bc in Output) bc.CompleteAdding();
    }
  }
}
```

4. Add the following code snippet inside the `Main` method:

```
var cts = new CancellationTokenSource();

Task.Run(() =>
{
  if (Console.ReadKey().KeyChar == 'c')
    cts.Cancel();
});

var sourceArrays = new BlockingCollection<int>[
  CollectionsNumber];
for (int i = 0; i < sourceArrays.Length; i++)
{
  sourceArrays[i] = new BlockingCollection<int>(Count);
}
```

```
var filter1 = new PipelineWorker<int, decimal>
(sourceArrays,
  (n) => Convert.ToDecimal(n * 0.97),
  cts.Token,
  "filter1"
);

var filter2 = new PipelineWorker<decimal, string>
(filter1.Output,
  (s) => String.Format("--{0}--", s),
  cts.Token,
  "filter2"
  );

var filter3 = new PipelineWorker<string, string>
(filter2.Output,
  (s) => Console.WriteLine("The final result is {0} on
    thread id {1}", s,
      Thread.CurrentThread.ManagedThreadId), cts.Token,
        "filter3");

try
{
  Parallel.Invoke(
    () =>
    {
      Parallel.For(0, sourceArrays.Length * Count,
        (j, state) =>
      {
        if (cts.Token.IsCancellationRequested)
        {
          state.Stop();
        }
        int k = BlockingCollection<int>.TryAddToAny(
          sourceArrays, j);
        if (k >= 0)
        {
          Console.WriteLine("added {0} to source data on
            thread id {1}", j,
              Thread.CurrentThread.ManagedThreadId);
          Thread.Sleep(TimeSpan.FromMilliseconds(100));
        }
      });
      foreach (var arr in sourceArrays)
      {
```

```
            arr.CompleteAdding();
          }
        },
        () => filter1.Run(),
        () => filter2.Run(),
        () => filter3.Run()
      );
    }
    catch (AggregateException ae)
    {
      foreach (var ex in ae.InnerExceptions)
        Console.WriteLine(ex.Message + ex.StackTrace);
    }

    if (cts.Token.IsCancellationRequested)
    {
      Console.WriteLine("Operation has been canceled!
        Press ENTER to exit.");
    }
    else
    {
      Console.WriteLine("Press ENTER to exit.");
    }
    Console.ReadLine();
```

5. Run the program.

How it works...

In the preceding example, we implement one of the most common parallel programming scenarios. Imagine that we have some data that has to pass through several computation stages, which take a significant amount of time. The latter computation requires the results of the former, so we cannot run them in parallel.

If we had only one item to process, there would not be many possibilities to enhance the performance. However, if we run many items through the set of same computation stages, we can use a Parallel Pipeline technique. This means that we do not have to wait until all items pass through the first computation stage to go to the next one. It is enough to have just one item that finishes the stage, we move it to the next stage, and meanwhile the next item is being processed by the previous stage, and so on. As a result, we almost have parallel processing shifted by a time required for the first item to pass through the first computation stage.

Here, we use four collections for each processing stage, illustrating that we can process every stage in parallel as well. The first step that we do is to provide a possibility to cancel the whole process by pressing the *C* key. We create a cancellation token and run a separate task to monitor the *C* key. Then, we define our pipeline. It consists of three main stages. The first stage is where we put the initial numbers on the first four collections that serve as the item source to the latter pipeline. This code is inside the `Parallel.For` loop, which in turn is inside the `Parallel.Invoke` statement, as we run all the stages in parallel; the initial stage runs in parallel as well.

The next stage is defining our pipeline elements. The logic is defined inside the `PipelineWorker` class. We initialize the worker with the input collection, provide a transformation function, and then run the worker in parallel with the other workers. This way we define two workers, or filters, because they filter the initial sequence. One of them turns an integer into a decimal value, and the second one turns a decimal to a string. Finally, the last worker just prints every incoming string to the console. Everywhere we provide a running thread ID to see how everything works. Besides this, we added artificial delays, so the items processing will be more natural, as we really use heavy computations.

As a result, we see the exact expected behavior. First, some items are being created on the initial collections. Then, we see that the first filter starts to process them, and as they are being processed, the second filter starts to work, and finally the item goes to the last worker that prints it to the console.

Implementing Parallel Pipeline with TPL DataFlow

This recipe shows how to implement a Parallel Pipeline pattern with the help of TPL DataFlow library.

Getting ready

To start with this recipe, you will need a running Visual Studio 2012. There are no other prerequisites. The source code for this recipe could be found at `7644_Code\Chapter10\Recipe3`.

How to do it...

To understand how to implement Parallel Pipeline with TPL DataFlow, perform the following steps:

1. Start Visual Studio 2012. Create a new C# **Console Application** project.

2. Add references to the **Microsoft TPL DataFlow** NuGet package.

   1. Right-click on the **References** folder in the project and select the **Manage NuGet Packages...** menu option.

   2. Now add your preferred references to the **Microsoft TPL DataFlow** NuGet package. You can use the search option in the **Manage NuGet Packages** dialog as follows:

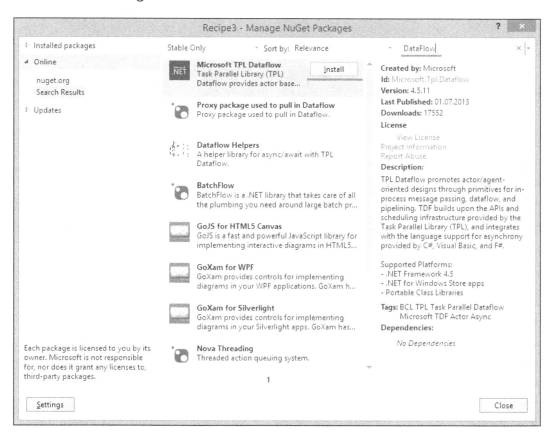

3. In the `Program.cs` file, add the following `using` directives:

```
using System;
using System.Threading;
using System.Threading.Tasks;
using System.Threading.Tasks.Dataflow;
```

4. Add the following code snippet below the `Main` method:

```
async static Task ProcessAsynchronously()
{
  var cts = new CancellationTokenSource();

  Task.Run(() =>
  {
    if (Console.ReadKey().KeyChar == 'c')
      cts.Cancel();
  });

  var inputBlock = new BufferBlock<int>(
    new DataflowBlockOptions { BoundedCapacity = 5,
      CancellationToken = cts.Token });

  var filter1Block = new TransformBlock<int, decimal>(
    n =>
    {
      decimal result = Convert.ToDecimal(n * 0.97);
      Console.WriteLine("Filter 1 sent {0} to the next
        stage on thread id {1}", result,
          Thread.CurrentThread.ManagedThreadId);
      Thread.Sleep(TimeSpan.FromMilliseconds(100));
      return result;
    },
    new ExecutionDataflowBlockOptions {
      MaxDegreeOfParallelism = 4, CancellationToken =
        cts.Token });

  var filter2Block = new TransformBlock<decimal, string>(
    n =>
    {
      string result = string.Format("--{0}--", n);
      Console.WriteLine("Filter 2 sent {0} to the next
        stage on thread id {1}", result,
          Thread.CurrentThread.ManagedThreadId);
      Thread.Sleep(TimeSpan.FromMilliseconds(100));
      return result;
    },
```

```
      new ExecutionDataflowBlockOptions {
       MaxDegreeOfParallelism = 4, CancellationToken =
         cts.Token });

   var outputBlock = new ActionBlock<string>(
     s =>
     {
       Console.WriteLine("The final result is {0} on thread
         id {1}", s, Thread.CurrentThread.ManagedThreadId);
     },
     new ExecutionDataflowBlockOptions {
       MaxDegreeOfParallelism = 4, CancellationToken =
         cts.Token });

   inputBlock.LinkTo(filter1Block, new DataflowLinkOptions {
     PropagateCompletion = true });
   filter1Block.LinkTo(filter2Block, new DataflowLinkOptions
     { PropagateCompletion = true });
   filter2Block.LinkTo(outputBlock, new DataflowLinkOptions
     { PropagateCompletion = true });

   try
   {
     Parallel.For(0, 20, new ParallelOptions {
       MaxDegreeOfParallelism = 4, CancellationToken =
         cts.Token }
     , i =>
     {
       Console.WriteLine("added {0} to source data on thread
         id {1}", i, Thread.CurrentThread.ManagedThreadId);
       inputBlock.SendAsync(i).GetAwaiter().GetResult();
     });
     inputBlock.Complete();
     await outputBlock.Completion;
     Console.WriteLine("Press ENTER to exit.");
   }
   catch (OperationCanceledException)
   {
     Console.WriteLine("Operation has been canceled!
       Press ENTER to exit.");
   }

   Console.ReadLine();
}
```

5. Add the following code snippet inside the `Main` method:

    ```
    var t = ProcessAsynchronously();
    t.GetAwaiter().GetResult();
    ```

6. Run the program.

How it works...

In the previous recipe, we have implemented a Parallel Pipeline pattern to process items through sequential stages. It is quite a common problem, and one of the proposed ways to program such algorithms is using a TPL DataFlow library from Microsoft. It is distributed via **NuGet**, and is easy to install and use in your application.

The TPL DataFlow library contains different type of blocks that can be connected with each other in different ways and form complicated processes that can be partially parallel and sequential where needed. To see some of the available infrastructure, let's implement the previous scenario with the help of the TPL DataFlow library.

First, we define the different blocks that will be processing our data. Please note that these blocks have different options that can be specified during their construction; they can be very important. For example, we pass the cancellation token into every block we define, and when we signal the cancellation, all of them will stop working.

We start our process with `BufferBlock`. This block holds items to pass it to the next blocks in the flow. We restrict it to the five-items capacity, specifying the `BoundedCapacity` option value. This means that when there will be five items in this block, it will stop accepting new items until one of the existing items pass to the next blocks.

The next block type is `TransformBlock`. This block is intended for a data transformation step. Here we define two transformation blocks, one of them creates decimals from integers, and the second one creates a string from a decimal value. There is a `MaxDegreeOfParallelism` option for this block, specifying the maximum simultaneous worker threads.

The last block is the `ActionBlock` type. This block will run a specified action on every incoming item. We use this block to print our items to the console.

Now, we link these blocks together with the help of the `LinkTo` methods. Here we have an easy sequential data flow, but it is possible to create schemes that are more complicated. Here we also provide `DataflowLinkOptions` with the `PropagateCompletion` property set to `true`. This means that when the step completes, it will automatically propagate its results and exceptions to the next stage. Then we start adding items to the buffer block in parallel, calling the block's `Complete` method, when we finish adding new items. Then we wait for the last block to complete. In case of a cancellation, we handle `OperationCancelledException` and cancel the whole process.

Implementing Map/Reduce with PLINQ

This recipe will describe how to implement the **Map/Reduce** pattern while using PLINQ.

Getting ready

To begin with this recipe, you will need a running Visual Studio 2012. There are no other prerequisites. The source code for this recipe can be found at `7644_Code\Chapter10\Recipe4`.

How to do it...

To understand how to implement Map/Reduce with PLINQ, perform the following steps:

1. Start Visual Studio 2012. Create a new C# **Console Application** project.

2. In the `Program.cs` file, add the following `using` directives:

```
using System;
using System.Collections.Generic;
using System.IO;
using System.Linq;
```

3. Add the following code snippet below the `Main` method:

```
private static readonly char[] delimiters =
  Enumerable.Range(0, 256).Select(i => (char)i).Where(c =>
    !char.IsLetterOrDigit(c)).ToArray();

private const string textToParse = @"
Call me Ishmael. Some years ago - never mind how long precisely -
having little or no money in my purse, and nothing particular to
interest me on shore, I thought I would sail about a little and
see the watery part of the world. It is a way I have of driving
off the spleen, and regulating the circulation. Whenever I find
myself growing grim about the mouth; whenever it is a damp,
drizzly November in my soul; whenever I find myself involuntarily
pausing before coffin warehouses, and bringing up the rear of
every funeral I meet; and especially whenever my hypos get such
an upper hand of me, that it requires a strong moral principle
to prevent me from deliberately stepping into the street, and
methodically knocking people's hats off - then, I account it high
time to get to sea as soon as I can.

⊠ Herman Melville, Moby Dick.
";
```

4. Add the following code snippet inside the `Main` method:

```
var q = textToParse.Split(delimiters)
  .AsParallel()
  .MapReduce(
    s => s.ToLower().ToCharArray()
  , c => c
  , g => new[] {new {Char = g.Key, Count = g.Count()}})
  .Where(c => char.IsLetterOrDigit(c.Char))
  .OrderByDescending( c => c.Count);

foreach (var info in q)
{
  Console.WriteLine("Character {0} occured in the text {1}
    {2}", info.Char, info.Count, info.Count == 1 ? "
      time" : "times");
}
Console.WriteLine(" -------------------------------------------");
const string searchPattern = "en";

var q2 = textToParse.Split(delimiters)
  .AsParallel()
  .Where(s => s.Contains(searchPattern))
  .MapReduce(
    s => new [] {s}
  , s => s
  , g => new[] {new {Word = g.Key, Count = g.Count()}})
  .OrderByDescending(s => s.Count);

Console.WriteLine("Words with search pattern '{0}':",
  searchPattern);
foreach (var info in q2)
{
  Console.WriteLine("{0} occured in the text {1} {2}",
    info.Word, info.Count,
    info.Count == 1 ? "time" : "times");
}

int halfLengthWordIndex = textToParse.IndexOf(' ',
  textToParse.Length/2);

using(var sw = File.CreateText("1.txt"))
{
  sw.Write(textToParse.Substring(0, halfLengthWordIndex));
}

using(var sw = File.CreateText("2.txt"))
{
```

```
      sw.Write(textToParse.Substring(halfLengthWordIndex));
   }

   string[] paths = new[] { ".\\" };

   Console.WriteLine(" -----------------------------------------------
   --");
   var q3 = paths
     .SelectMany(p => Directory.EnumerateFiles(p, "*.txt"))
     .AsParallel()
     .MapReduce(
       path => File.ReadLines(path).SelectMany(line =>
         line.Trim(delimiters).Split(delimiters)),
           word => string.IsNullOrWhiteSpace(word) ? '\t' :
             word.ToLower()[0], g => new [] { new {
               FirstLetter = g.Key, Count = g.Count()}})
     .Where(s => char.IsLetterOrDigit(s.FirstLetter))
     .OrderByDescending(s => s.Count);

   Console.WriteLine("Words from text files");

   foreach (var info in q3)
   {
     Console.WriteLine("Words starting with letter '{0}'
       occured in the text {1} {2}", info.FirstLetter,
         info.Count,
       info.Count == 1 ? "time" : "times");
   }
```

5. Add the following code snippet after the `Program` class definition:

```
static class PLINQExtensions
{
  public static ParallelQuery<TResult> MapReduce<TSource,
    TMapped, TKey, TResult>(
    this ParallelQuery<TSource> source,
    Func<TSource, IEnumerable<TMapped>> map,
    Func<TMapped, TKey> keySelector,
    Func<IGrouping<TKey, TMapped>,
    IEnumerable<TResult>> reduce)
  {
    return source.SelectMany(map)
    .GroupBy(keySelector)
    .SelectMany(reduce);
  }
}
```

6. Run the program.

How it works...

The `Map/Reduce` functions are another important parallel programming pattern. It is suitable for a small program and large multi-server computations. The meaning of this pattern is that you have two special functions to apply to your data. The first of them is the `Map` function. It takes a set of initial data in a key/value list form and produces another key/value sequence, transforming the data to the comfortable format for further processing. Then we use another function called `Reduce`. The `Reduce` function takes the result of the `Map` function and transforms it to a smallest possible set of data that we actually need. To understand how this algorithm works, let's look through the recipe.

First, we define a relatively large text in the string variable: `textToParse`. We need this text to run our queries on. Then we define our `Map/Reduce` implementation as a PLINQ extension method in the `PLINQExtensions` class. We use `SelectMany` to transform the initial sequence to the sequence we need by applying the `Map` function. This function produces several new elements from one sequence element. Then we choose how we group the new sequence with the `keySelector` function, and we use `GroupBy` with this key to produce an intermediate key/value sequence. The last thing we do is applying `Reduce` to the resulting grouped sequence to get the result.

In our first example, we split the text into separate words, and then we chop each word into character sequences with the help of the `Map` function, and group the result by the character value. The `Reduce` function finally transforms the sequence into a key value pair, where we have a character and a number for the times it was used in the text ordered by the usage. Therefore, we are able to count each character appearance in the text in parallel (since we use PLINQ to query the initial data).

The next example is quite similar, but now we use PLINQ to filter the sequence leaving only the words containing our search pattern, and we then get all those words sorted by their usage in the text.

Finally, the last example uses file I/O. We save the sample text on the disk, splitting it into two files. Then we define the `Map` function as producing a number of strings from the directory name, which are all the words from all the lines in all text files in the initial directory. Then we group those words by the first letter (filtering out the empty strings) and use reduce to see which letter is most often used as the first word letter in the text. What is nice is that we can easily change this program to be distributed by just using other implementations of map and reduce functions, and we still are able to use PLINQ with them to make our program easy to read and maintain.

11

There's More

In this chapter, we will look through a new programming paradigm in the Windows 8 operating system. You will learn about:

- Using a timer in a Windows Store application
- Using WinRT from a usual application
- Using BackgroundTask in a Windows Store application

Introduction

Microsoft released the first public beta build of Windows 8 at the BUILD conference on September 13, 2011. The new OS tried to address almost every problem that Windows had by introducing features such as responsive UI suitable for tablet devices with touch, lower power consumption, new application model, new asynchronous APIs, and tighter security.

The core of Windows API improvements was a new multiplatform component system, **WinRT**, which is a logical development of COM. With WinRT, a programmer can use native C++ code, C# and .NET, and even JavaScript and HTML to develop applications. Another change is the introduction of a centralized application store, which did not exist on the Windows platform before.

Being a new application platform, Windows 8 had backward-compatibility and allowed to run the usual Windows applications. This lead to a situation where there are two major classes of applications: the Windows Store applications, where new programs are distributed via the Windows Store, and the usual classic applications that did not change since the previous version of Windows.

The Windows Store applications are what we are going to look at in this chapter. The development paradigm shifted very much, and as a programmer you have to comply with specific rules. The program has to respond in a limited time to start up or to finish, keeping the whole operating system and other applications responsive. To save the battery, your applications are no longer running in the background by default; instead of that they get suspended and actually stop executing.

New Windows APIs are asynchronous, and you can use only white-listed API functions in your application. For example, you are not allowed to create a new `Thread` class instance anymore. You have to use a system-managed thread pool instead. A lot of usual APIs cannot be used anymore, and you have to study new ways to achieve the same goals as before.

In this chapter, we will see how a Windows Store application is different from the usual Windows application, how we can use some of the WinRT benefits from the usual applications, and go through a simplified scenario of a Windows Store application with background notifications.

Using a timer in a Windows Store application

This recipe shows how to use a simple timer in Windows Store applications.

Getting ready

To step through this recipe, you will need Visual Studio 2012 and the Windows 8+ operating system. No other prerequisites are required. The source code for this recipe can be found at `7644_Code\Chapter11\Recipe1`.

How to do it...

To understand how to use a timer in a Windows Store application, perform the following steps:

1. Start Visual Studio 2012. Create a new C# **Blank App (XAML)** project under **Windows Store**.

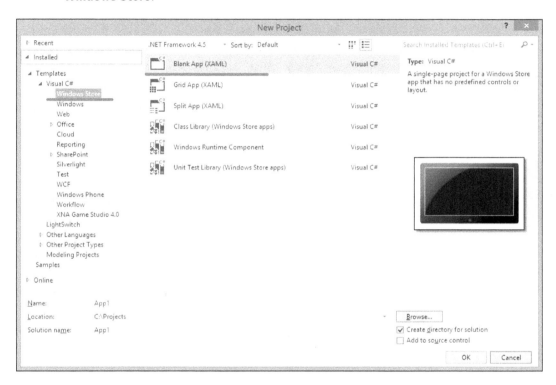

2. In case you are asked to renew your developer license, you have to agree to the Microsoft privacy terms.

3. Then, sign in to your Microsoft account (or create one first).

4. Finally, you get a confirmation dialog that the developer license was successfully renewed.

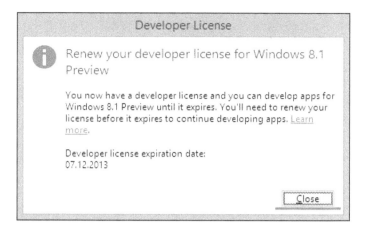

5. In the `MainPage.xaml` file, add the `Name` attribute to the `Grid` element:

```
<Grid Name="Grid" Background="{StaticResource
    ApplicationPageBackgroundThemeBrush}">
```

6. In the `MainPage.xaml.cs` file, add the following `using` directives:

```
using System;
using Windows.UI.Xaml;
using Windows.UI.Xaml.Controls;
using Windows.UI.Xaml.Navigation;
```

7. Add the following code snippet above the `MainPage` constructor definition:

```
private readonly DispatcherTimer _timer;
private int _ticks;
```

8. Replace the `MainPage()` constructor with the following code snippet:

```
public MainPage()
{
    InitializeComponent();
    _timer = new DispatcherTimer();
    _ticks = 0;
}
```

9. Add the following code snippet inside the `OnNavigatedTo` method:

```
Grid.Children.Clear();
var commonPanel = new StackPanel
{
  Orientation = Orientation.Vertical,
  HorizontalAlignment = HorizontalAlignment.Center
};

var buttonPanel = new StackPanel
{
  Orientation = Orientation.Horizontal,
  HorizontalAlignment = HorizontalAlignment.Center
};

var textBlock = new TextBlock
{
  Text = "Sample timer application",
  FontSize = 32,
  HorizontalAlignment = HorizontalAlignment.Center,
  Margin = new Thickness(40)
};

var timerTextBlock = new TextBlock
{
  Text = "0",
  FontSize = 32,
  HorizontalAlignment = HorizontalAlignment.Center,
  Margin = new Thickness(40)
};

var timerStateTextBlock = new TextBlock
{
  Text = "Timer is enabled",
  FontSize = 32,
  HorizontalAlignment = HorizontalAlignment.Center,
  Margin = new Thickness(40)
};

var startButton = new Button { Content = "Start",
  FontSize = 32};
var stopButton = new Button { Content = "Stop",
  FontSize = 32};

buttonPanel.Children.Add(startButton);
buttonPanel.Children.Add(stopButton);
```

```
commonPanel.Children.Add(textBlock);
commonPanel.Children.Add(timerTextBlock);
commonPanel.Children.Add(timerStateTextBlock);
commonPanel.Children.Add(buttonPanel);

_timer.Interval = TimeSpan.FromSeconds(1);
_timer.Tick += (sender, eventArgs) =>
{
  timerTextBlock.Text = _ticks.ToString(); _ticks++;
};
_timer.Start();

startButton.Click += (sender, eventArgs) =>
{
  timerTextBlock.Text = "0";
  _timer.Start();
  _ticks = 1;
  timerStateTextBlock.Text = "Timer is enabled";
};

stopButton.Click += (sender, eventArgs) =>
{
  _timer.Stop();
  timerStateTextBlock.Text = "Timer is disabled";
};

Grid.Children.Add(commonPanel);
```

10. Run the program.

How it works...

When the program runs, it creates an instance of a `MainPage` class. Here we instantiate `DispatcherTimer` in the constructor, and initialize the `ticks` counter to zero. Then, in the `OnNavigatedTo` event handler, we create our UI controls and bind the start and stop buttons to the corresponding lambda expressions, which contain the `start` and `stop` logics.

As you can see, the `timer` event handler works directly with the UI controls. This is okay because `DispatcherTimer` is implemented in such a way that the handlers of the `Tick` event of `timer` are run by the UI thread. However, if you run the program and then switch to something else, and switch the to the program delete after a couple of minutes, you may notice that the seconds counter is far behind the real amount of time passed. This happens because Windows 8 applications, or Windows Store applications as they are usually referred to, have completely different lifecycles.

Please be aware that Windows Store applications behave much like the applications on smartphone and tablet platforms. Instead of running in the background they become suspended after some time, and this means that they are actually frozen until the user switches back to them. You have a limited time to save the current application state before it becomes suspended, and you are able to restore the state when the applications run again.

While this behavior could save power and CPU resources, it creates significant difficulties to program applications that are supposed to do some processing in the background. Windows 8 has a set of special APIs for programming such applications. We will go through such a scenario later in this chapter.

Using WinRT from usual applications

This recipe shows how to create a console application that will be able to use the WinRT API.

Getting ready

To step through this recipe, you will need Visual Studio 2012 and the Windows 8+ operating system. There are no other prerequisites. The source code for this recipe can be found at `7644_Code\Chapter11\Recipe2`.

How to do it...

To understand how to use WinRT from usual applications, perform the following steps:

1. Start Visual Studio 2012. Create a new C# **Console Application** project.

2. Right-click on the created project in Visual Studio **Solution Explorer** and select the **Unload Project...** menu option.

3. Right-click on the unloaded project and select the **Edit ProjectName.csproj** menu option.

4. Add the following XML below the `<TargetFrameworkVersion>` element:

   `<TargetPlatformVersion>8.0</TargetPlatformVersion>`

5. Save the `.csproj` file, right-click on the unloaded project in Visual Studio **Solution Explorer**, and select the **Reload Project** menu option.

6. Right-click on the project and select **Add Reference** from the **Core** library under **Windows**. Then click on the **Browse** button.

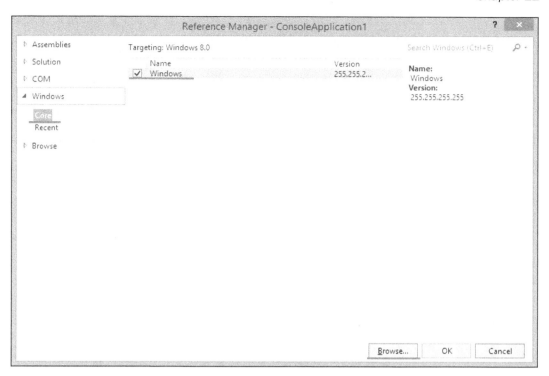

7. Navigate to `C:\Program Files\Reference Assemblies\Microsoft\Framework\.NETCore\v4.5` and click on `System.Runtime.WindowsRuntime.dll`.

8. In the `Program.cs` file add the following `using` directives:

```
using System;
using System.IO;
using System.Threading.Tasks;
using Windows.Storage;
```

9. Add the following code snippet below the `Main` method:

```
async static Task AsynchronousProcessing()
{
  StorageFolder folder = KnownFolders.DocumentsLibrary;

  if (await folder.DoesFileExistAsync("test.txt"))
  {
    var fileToDelete = await folder.GetFileAsync(
      "test.txt");
```

```
      await fileToDelete.DeleteAsync(
        StorageDeleteOption.PermanentDelete);
    }

    var file = await folder.CreateFileAsync("test.txt",
      CreationCollisionOption.ReplaceExisting);
    using (var stream = await file.OpenAsync(FileAccessMode.
ReadWrite))
      using (var writer = new StreamWriter(stream.AsStreamForWrite()))
      {
        await writer.WriteLineAsync("Test content");
        await writer.FlushAsync();
      }

    using (var stream = await file.OpenAsync(FileAccessMode.Read))
      using (var reader = new StreamReader(stream.AsStreamForRead()))
      {
        string content = await reader.ReadToEndAsync();
        Console.WriteLine(content);
      }

    Console.WriteLine("Enumerating Folder Structure:");

    var itemsList = await folder.GetItemsAsync();
    foreach (var item in itemsList)
    {
      if (item is StorageFolder)
      {
        Console.WriteLine("{0} folder", item.Name);
      }
      else
      {
        Console.WriteLine(item.Name);
      }
    }
  }
```

10. Add the following code snippet inside the `Main` method:

```
var t = AsynchronousProcessing();
t.GetAwaiter().GetResult();
Console.WriteLine();
Console.WriteLine("Press ENTER to continue");
Console.ReadLine();
```

11. Add the following code snippet below the `Program` class definition:

```
static class Extensions
{
  public static async Task<bool> DoesFileExistAsync(this
    StorageFolder folder, string fileName)
  {
    try
    {
      await folder.GetFileAsync(fileName);
      return true;
    }
    catch (FileNotFoundException)
    {
      return false;
    }
  }
}
```

12. Run the program.

How it works...

Here we used quite a tricky way to consume the WinRT API from a common .NET console application. Unfortunately, not all available APIs will work in that scenario, but still it could be useful to work with movement sensors, GPS location services, and so on.

To reference WinRT in Visual Studio we manually edit the `.csproj` file specifying the target platform for the application as Windows 8. Then we manually reference `System.Runtime.WindowsRuntime.dll` to leverage the `GetAwaiter` extension method implementation for the WinRT asynchronous operations. This allows us to use `await` on WinRT APIs directly. There is a backward conversion as well. When we create a WinRT library, we have to expose the WinRT native `IAsyncOperation` interfaces family for asynchronous operations, so they could be consumed from JavaScript and C++ in a language-agnostic manner.

File operations in WinRT are quite self-descriptive; here we have asynchronous file create and delete operations. Still, file operations in WinRT contain security restrictions, encouraging you to use special Windows folders for your application, and not allowing you to work with just any file path on your disk drive.

Using BackgroundTask in Windows Store applications

This recipe walks through the process of creating a background task in a Windows Store application, which updates the application's live tile on a desktop.

Getting ready

To step through this recipe, you will need Visual Studio 2012 and the Windows 8+ operating system. There are no other prerequisites. The source code for this recipe can be found at `7644_Code\Chapter11\Recipe3`.

How to do it...

To understand how to use `BackgroundTask` in Windows Store applications, perform the following steps:

1. Start Visual Studio 2012. Create a new C# **Blank App (XAML)** project under **Windows Store**. In case you need to renew a developer license, please refer to the *Using a timer in a Windows Store application* recipe for detailed instructions.

2. In the **Assets** folder, open the **SmallLogo.png** file in the Paint editor, crop it to the 24 x 24 pixels size, save it back to the **Assets** folder as `SmallLogo-Badge.png`, and include it in the project.

3. Open the `Package.appxmanifest` file. In the **Declarations** tab, add
   Background Tasks to **Supported Declarations**. Under **Properties**, check the
   supported properties **System event** and **Timer**, and set the name of **Entry point**
   to `YourNamespace.TileSchedulerTask`. `YourNamespace` should be the
   namespace of your application.

Application UI	Capabilities	Declarations	Packaging

Use this page to add declarations and specify their properties.

Available Declarations:

Background Tasks | Add |

Supported Declarations:

Background Tasks | Remove |

Description:

Enables the app to specify the class name of an in-proc server DLL that runs the ap
in response to external trigger events. The class hosted in the in-proc server DLL is
activation, and its Run method is invoked.

Multiple instances of this declaration are allowed in each app.

More information

Properties:

Supported task types

☐ Audio

☐ Control channel

☑ System event

☑ Timer

☐ Push notification

App settings

Executable:

Entry point: WinRTClockCustom2.TileSchedulerTask

Start page:

4. In the **Application UI** tab, select **Lock screen notifications** as **Badge**, and **Badge logo** as **Assets\SmallLogo-Badge.png**.

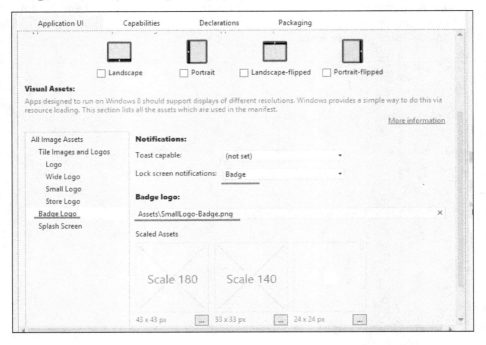

5. In the `MainPage.xaml` file, insert the following XAML into the `Grid` element:

```
<StackPanel Margin="50">
  <TextBlock Name="Clock"
             Text="HH:mm"
             HorizontalAlignment="Center"
             VerticalAlignment="Center"
             Style="{StaticResource HeaderTextStyle}"/>
</StackPanel>
```

6. In the `MainPage.xaml.cs` file add the following `using` directives:

```
using System;
using System.Diagnostics;
using System.Globalization;
using System.Linq;
using System.Xml.Linq;
using Windows.ApplicationModel.Background;
using Windows.Data.Xml.Dom;
using Windows.System.UserProfile;
using Windows.UI.Notifications;
using Windows.UI.Xaml;
using Windows.UI.Xaml.Controls;
using Windows.UI.Xaml.Navigation;
```

7. Add the following code snippet above the `MainPage` constructor definition:

```
private const string TASK_NAME_USERPRESENT =
  "TileSchedulerTask_UserPresent";
private const string TASK_NAME_TIMER =
  "TileSchedulerTask_Timer";

private readonly CultureInfo _cultureInfo;
private readonly DispatcherTimer _timer;
```

8. Replace the `MainPage` constructor with the following code snippet:

```
public MainPage()
{
InitializeComponent();

string language = GlobalizationPreferences.Languages.First();
_cultureInfo = new CultureInfo(language);

_timer = new DispatcherTimer();
_timer.Interval = TimeSpan.FromSeconds(1);
_timer.Tick += (sender, e) => UpdateClockText();
}
```

9. Add the following code snippet above the `OnNavigatedTo` method:

```
private void UpdateClockText()
{
  Clock.Text = DateTime.Now.ToString(
    _cultureInfo.DateTimeFormat.FullDateTimePattern);
}

private static async void CreateClockTask()
{
  BackgroundAccessStatus result = await
    BackgroundExecutionManager.RequestAccessAsync();
  if (result == BackgroundAccessStatus.
    AllowedMayUseActiveRealTimeConnectivity ||
      result == BackgroundAccessStatus.
        AllowedWithAlwaysOnRealTimeConnectivity)
  {
    TileSchedulerTask.CreateSchedule();

    EnsureUserPresentTask();
    EnsureTimerTask();
  }
}

private static void EnsureUserPresentTask()
{
```

```
      foreach (var task in BackgroundTaskRegistration.AllTasks)
        if (task.Value.Name == TASK_NAME_USERPRESENT)
          return;

      var builder = new BackgroundTaskBuilder();
      builder.Name = TASK_NAME_USERPRESENT;
      builder.TaskEntryPoint =
        (typeof(TileSchedulerTask)).FullName;
      builder.SetTrigger(new SystemTrigger(
        SystemTriggerType.UserPresent, false));
      builder.Register();
    }

    private static void EnsureTimerTask()
    {
      foreach (var task in BackgroundTaskRegistration.AllTasks)
        if (task.Value.Name == TASK_NAME_TIMER)
          return;

      var builder = new BackgroundTaskBuilder();
      builder.Name = TASK_NAME_TIMER;
      builder.TaskEntryPoint = (typeof(
        TileSchedulerTask)).FullName;
      builder.SetTrigger(new TimeTrigger(180, false));
      builder.Register();
    }
```

10. Add the following code snippet inside the `OnNavigatedTo` method:

```
_timer.Start();
UpdateClockText();
CreateClockTask();
```

11. Add the following code snippet below the `MainPage` class definition:

```
public sealed class TileSchedulerTask : IBackgroundTask
{
  public void Run(IBackgroundTaskInstance taskInstance)
  {
    var deferral = taskInstance.GetDeferral();
    CreateSchedule();
    deferral.Complete();
  }

  public static void CreateSchedule()
  {
```

```csharp
    var tileUpdater = TileUpdateManager.
CreateTileUpdaterForApplication();
    var plannedUpdated = tileUpdater.
GetScheduledTileNotifications();

    DateTime now = DateTime.Now;
    DateTime planTill = now.AddHours(4);

    DateTime updateTime = new DateTime(now.Year, now.Month,
      now.Day, now.Hour, now.Minute, 0).AddMinutes(1);
    if (plannedUpdated.Count > 0)
      updateTime = plannedUpdated.Select(x =>
        x.DeliveryTime.DateTime).Union(new[] { updateTime
          }).Max();
    XmlDocument documentNow = GetTilenotificationXml(now);

    tileUpdater.Update(new TileNotification(documentNow) {
      ExpirationTime = now.AddMinutes(1) });

    for (var startPlanning = updateTime;
      startPlanning < planTill; startPlanning =
        startPlanning.AddMinutes(1))
    {
      Debug.WriteLine(startPlanning);
      Debug.WriteLine(planTill);

      try
      {
        XmlDocument document = GetTilenotificationXml(
          startPlanning);

        var scheduledNotification = new
          ScheduledTileNotification(document,
            new DateTimeOffset(startPlanning))
        {
          ExpirationTime = startPlanning.AddMinutes(1)
        };

        tileUpdater.AddToSchedule(scheduledNotification);
      }
      catch (Exception ex)
      {
        Debug.WriteLine("Error: " + ex.Message);
      }
    }
  }

  private static XmlDocument GetTilenotificationXml(
    DateTime dateTime)
  {
```

```
        string language =
          GlobalizationPreferences.Languages.First();
        var cultureInfo = new CultureInfo(language);

        string shortDate = dateTime.ToString(
          cultureInfo.DateTimeFormat.ShortTimePattern);
        string longDate = dateTime.ToString(
          cultureInfo.DateTimeFormat.LongDatePattern);

        var document = XElement.Parse(string.Format(@"<tile>
        <visual>
          <binding template=""TileSquareText02"">
            <text id=""1"">{0}</text>
            <text id=""2"">{1}</text>
          </binding>
          <binding template=""TileWideText01"">
            <text id=""1"">{0}</text>
            <text id=""2"">{1}</text>
            <text id=""3""></text>
            <text id=""4""></text>
          </binding>
        </visual>
      </tile>", shortDate, longDate));

        return document.ToXmlDocument();
      }
    }

    public static class DocumentExtensions
    {
      public static XmlDocument ToXmlDocument(this
        XElement xDocument)
      {
        var xmlDocument = new XmlDocument();
        xmlDocument.LoadXml(xDocument.ToString());
        return xmlDocument;
      }
    }
```

12. Run the program.

How it works...

The preceding program shows how to create a background time-based task, and how to show the updates from this task on a live tile on the Windows 8 start screen. Programming Windows Store applications is quite a challenging task itself—you have to care about an application suspending/restoring its state, and many other things. Here we are going to concentrate on our main task, leaving behind the secondary issues.

Our main goal is to run some code, when the application itself is not in the foreground. First, we create an implementation of the `IBackgroundTask` interface. This is our code, and the `Run` method will be called when we get a trigger signal. It is important that if the `Run` method contains asynchronous code with `await` in it, we have to use a special deferral object as shown in the recipe to explicitly specify when we begin and end the `Run` method execution. In our case, method call is synchronous, but to illustrate this requirement we work with the deferral object.

Inside our task in the `Run` method, we create a set of tile updates each minute for 4 hours, and register it in `TileUpdateManager` with the help of the `ScheduledTaskNotification` class. A tile uses a special XML format to specify how exactly the text should be positioned on it. When we trigger our task from the system, it schedules one-minute tile updates for the next 4 hours. Then, we need to register our background task. We do it twice; one registration provides a `UserPresent` trigger, which means that this task will be triggered when a user is logged on. The next trigger is a time trigger, which runs the task once every 3 hours.

When the program runs, it creates a timer, which runs when the application is in the foreground. At the same time it is trying to register background tasks; to register those tasks the program needs user permission, and it will show a dialog requesting permissions from the user. Now we have scheduled live tile updates for the next 4 hours. If we close our application, the live tile will continue to show new time every minute. In the next 3 hours the time trigger will run our background task once again, and we will schedule another live tile update.

Index

Thank you for buying
Multithreading in C# 5.0 Cookbook

About Packt Publishing

Packt, pronounced 'packed', published its first book "*Mastering phpMyAdmin for Effective MySQL Management*" in April 2004 and subsequently continued to specialize in publishing highly focused books on specific technologies and solutions.

Our books and publications share the experiences of your fellow IT professionals in adapting and customizing today's systems, applications, and frameworks. Our solution based books give you the knowledge and power to customize the software and technologies you're using to get the job done. Packt books are more specific and less general than the IT books you have seen in the past. Our unique business model allows us to bring you more focused information, giving you more of what you need to know, and less of what you don't.

Packt is a modern, yet unique publishing company, which focuses on producing quality, cutting-edge books for communities of developers, administrators, and newbies alike. For more information, please visit our website: www.packtpub.com.

Writing for Packt

We welcome all inquiries from people who are interested in authoring. Book proposals should be sent to author@packtpub.com. If your book idea is still at an early stage and you would like to discuss it first before writing a formal book proposal, contact us; one of our commissioning editors will get in touch with you.

We're not just looking for published authors; if you have strong technical skills but no writing experience, our experienced editors can help you develop a writing career, or simply get some additional reward for your expertise.

Learning C# by Developing Games with Unity 3D Beginner's Guide

ISBN: 978-1-84969-658-6   Paperback: 292 pages

Learn the fundamentals of C# to create scripts for your GameObjects

1. You've actually been creating scripts in your mind your whole life, you just didn't realize it. Apply this logical ability to write Unity C# scripts

2. Learn how to use the two primary building blocks for writing scripts: the variable and the method. They're not mysterious or intimidating, just a simple form of substitution

3. Learn about GameObjects and Component objects as well as the vital communication between these objects using Dot Syntax. It's easy, just like addressing a postal letter

---

Boost C++ Application Development Cookbook

ISBN: 978-1-84951-488-0   Paperback: 348 pages

Over 80 practical, task-based recipes to create applications using Boost libraries

1. Explores how to write a program once and then use it on Linux, Windows, MacOS, and Android operating systems

2. Includes everyday use recipes for multithreading, networking, metaprogramming, and generic programming from a Boost library developer

3. Take advantage of the real power of Boost and C++ to get a good grounding in using it in any project

Please check **www.PacktPub.com** for information on our titles

Visual Studio 2012 and .NET 4.5
Expert Development Cookbook

Abhishek Sur

Visual Studio 2012 and .NET 4.5 Expert Development Cookbook

ISBN: 978-1-84968-670-9   Paperback: 380 pages

Over 40 recipes for successfully mixing the powerful capabilities of .NET 4.5 and Visual Studio 2012

1. Step-by-step instructions to learn the power of .NET development with Visual Studio 2012

2. Filled with examples that clearly illustrate how to integrate with the technologies and frameworks of your choice

3. Each sample demonstrates key conceptsto build your knowledge of the architecture in a practical and incremental way

.NET 4.5 Parallel
Extensions Cookbook

Bryan Freeman

.NET 4.5 Parallel Extensions Cookbook

ISBN: 978-1-84969-022-5   Paperback: 336 pages

80 recipes to create scalable, task-based parallel programs using .NET 4.5

1. Create multithreaded applications using .NET Framework 4.5

2. Get introduced to .NET 4.5 parallel extensions and familiarized with .NET parallel loops

3. Use new data structures introduced by .NET Framework 4.5 to simplify complex synchronisation problems

4. Practical recipes on everything you will need to create task-based parallel programs

Please check **www.PacktPub.com** for information on our titles

www.ingramcontent.com/pod-product-compliance
Lightning Source LLC
LaVergne TN
LVHW062310060326
832902LV00013B/2149